Clutter Control

Jeff Campbell is the unrivalled master of modern home cleaning and organization. In 1979 he founded The Clean Team, probably San Francisco's busiest and most popular house-cleaning service. Jeff Campbell and The Clean Team whip an entire house into shape in forty-two minutes flat. Despite the fact that he actually enjoys cleaning, especially when he gets paid for it, his philosophy has always been that we all have better things to do with our weekends than clean the house. He is a co-founder of a house-cleaning franchise, and is hard at work teaching franchisees how to operate a successful house-cleaning service. He lives in California.

D0281005

Clutter Control

JEFF CAMPBELL

ROBERT HALE · LONDON

© *Jeff Campbell 1992 & 1997*
This edition first published in Great Britain 1997
by arrangement with Bantam Doubleday Dell Publishing Group, Inc., USA

ISBN 0 7090 6160 9

Robert Hale Limited
Clerkenwell House
Clerkenwell Green
London EC1R 0HT

The right of Jeff Campbell to be identified as
author of this work has been asserted by him
in accordance with the Copyright, Designs and
Patents Act 1988.

2 4 6 8 10 9 7 5 3 1

Typeset by
Derek Doyle & Associates, Mold, Flintshire
Printed by
St Edmundsbury Press Limited, Bury St Edmunds, Suffolk
Bound by
WBC Book Manufacturers Limited, Bridgend

Contents

Acknowledgements

Bill Redican helped write and rewrite this project. He also called upon his educational roots as a Ph.D. research psychologist to illuminate us on the psychology of clutter in Chapter 2. Thank you – again.

Charlene Richter, president of Getting Organized, in San Francisco, was kind enough to share her expert knowledge of clutter-bashing tactics both in person and through her Learning Annex class. She also works as an individual clutter consultant. Thank you.

Mike Curry, Sean Hyland, and my other friends and partners at The Clean Team kept things going even after a fire on St Patrick's Day destroyed our office building. You all did what you had to do, and then you did some more. Thank you.

In memory of Wally and Ann

Introduction

Ask a dozen people what drives them crazy around their house – apart from their partner, of course – and the chances are most will mention clutter high on the list: it's a universal irritant.

The consequences of clutter are lamentably too familiar:

- You can't find things, and you waste time looking for them, over and over again.
- Any sense of beauty or order in a room is out of the question.
- You're continually stymied trying to complete simple daily tasks.
- You can't even begin to clean the house.
- Your living space is uncomfortable and depressing.
- You're surrounded by evidence of what a colossal failure at housekeeping you appear to be.
- The house is too much of a mess to have friends to visit, and when they do 'pop over', it's humiliating.

· You're perpetually living in the past, and never have a sense of catching up with the present.

· Certain accumulations in your home can be a fire hazard or even a health hazard.

It's pretty clear that clutter is the bane of many existences. But what is the nature of this beast? The root of the word *clutter* is Middle English *clot* – a lump. Just as a blood clot stops the flow of vitality in the body, so household clutter blocks the proper flow of a home.

To us, clutter appears to involve one or both of two undesirable events. One of them is related to things. You have too much stuff, and/or the stuff you have is in a state of chaos. As we become a more affluent and object-oriented culture, the accumulation of more and better stuff is a phenomenon that has become a way of life. It's difficult to limit and organize this accumulation. The other undesirable event is related to time: interruptions of it, not enough of it, and not knowing where to start.

To some people, household clutter is all those things that get in the way – especially when trying to clean or organize, or to prepare for a visitor. To others, clutter is the relentlessly growing mountains of paper in their house – bills, post, magazines, newspapers, recipes, invoices, receipts, notes, lists, and scraps of paper that accumulate faster than they can be read, filed, paid, given away, or discarded. For other people, clutter is mostly an organizational problem – the *lack* of a system for paying bills, keeping appointments, or arranging the cupboards or drawers so things can be successfully and painlessly retrieved once they've been put away. And for you it may be the wardrobes filled to overflowing (but nothing ready to wear), or the packed bookshelves (but nothing new to read), or the garage (where it's nearly impossible to find anything or cram anything else into, let alone the car).

For many, what's annoying about clutter is the lost time caused by it – starting with the wasted time looking for misplaced things, but also including the cluttered feeling caused by too many things to do in the time available, and the clutter of interruptions when you finally find the time to try to get something done. Clutter even has a financial impact if you pay for storing stuff you never use, if you buy things you'll never need, if you end up buying more of something you already have an ample supply of – or if you come home from a tiring and time-consuming shopping trip without the most important item you went to the store to get in the first place.

No matter how we're personally afflicted by clutter, most of us already have some idea what to do about it. If you have too much stuff, it doesn't take a rocket scientist to figure out that you'll have to reduce the volume of it in some way. But even after you've got rid of as much as you're willing to, you've still got to organize what's left, or the mountain starts to grow again.

The idea is to take the germ of the solution that you already know, feed it, give it light and air, and let it bloom. That's one of the goals of this book – to give you confidence and encouragement – to move you to action so you put your hunches to work. In addition we'll fill in the gaps with some field-tested remedies – a team approach in which you'll get all the credit!

In the meantime, your stuff is driving you up the wall. You already know that having a garage or car-boot sale would be a good idea. But not only haven't you had one, you still don't have the will power to resist other people's sales. More stuff! Just what you need! And your house looks more and more like the flea markets you try to avoid. Even if you've managed to get everything in sight tucked away, do you know what's in your cupboards, cabinets, drawers, and garage? Heck, no!

Don't torment yourself if you're a clutterer. You're not alone. And this situation isn't a lot different from trying to lose a few pounds. People who are overweight certainly know that it would be helpful to change their eating behaviour and to exercise more. However, just being armed with these sterling facts does not make the pounds drop off in awe. The hard work is putting what you know into practice. That's why diet books are so popular. Many, many people would dearly love to find a system that makes losing weight easy and palatable: something –anything – that will take the work out of losing weight. Or that will deliver the will power neces- sary for the undertaking. Or that will give us the encour- agement we need. Or that will just teach us how to prepare food that tastes so good we'll hardly notice we're dieting.

Likewise with clutter. Getting rid of clutter is like putting your house on a diet. But just wanting to get rid of it won't make it happen. It can be painful to let go of our material goods. We may view them as a reflection of our lives and of our very impact while here on earth. They enhance our feelings of self-worth and security. They can represent our memories of family, loved ones, and days gone by.

So a big part of ourselves may not want any part of a household uncluttering project, thank you, despite the fact that the clutter is driving us crazy. At some level, uncluttering appears to be asking us to throw a chunk of ourselves away. Hence one of the reasons for an impasse over clutter. It torments us and we have a good idea of what to do about it, yet remedies appear to threaten some basic feelings about ourselves and our world. So we do nothing –but watch, helplessly, as the clutter, in blissful ignorance, piles higher and spreads wider.

What you're passing up by clinging to all this stuff are a number of substantial pay-offs: a wonderful sense of freedom; an ability (and the time) to manage your daily life; a capacity to live more in the present; an appreciation of a more beautiful home environment; and a more productive life. Imagine how great it would be if you didn't have the feeling that your home is running you instead of the other way around. Imagine everything in your home being in its right place. Imagine that you could find something when you needed it – not after an exasperating search or by accident a week later. Imagine that your filing system allowed you to schedule and keep your appointments, pay your bills in a timely fashion, and keep the flow of paper smooth. The liberating feelings of accomplishment and relief that come with banishing clutter are tangible, real, and healthy.

But you already knew that. And you're probably adult enough to know that life requires sensible compromises – among them ones that will enable you to shift from living the way you do now to living the way you would prefer.

Grand! You say you're quite prepared to compromise, to change some habits so you can get the clutter under control. There's one additional roadblock: inertia. We could all do with some encouragement to get the ball rolling, the necessary dose of will power to take action. It's the same mind-set achieved just before starting a successful diet or exercise programme. If you can see that there are direct and practical steps you can take to unclutter your home, and that you're far from being alone in this endeavour, you'll be more likely to feel that you can succeed.

Is it any wonder you're having such a hard time getting started? Besides all the motivational factors, you haven't been trained in organizing. Even if you took Home Economics, household organization probably wasn't taught during the course. How do you set about organizing a wardrobe, for example? What do you do first? If you're like many people, you don't even particularly want to be trained in organizing. You just want instant results (like an organized wardrobe). And some direct answers. That's our job – to give you direct and practical answers to questions about how to unclutter and organize your household wherever it's bothering you.

How do you know that you have a household clutter problem? We're not going to give you one of those self-scoring tests that you're doomed to fail. But here are a few questions you might want to ask yourself in a benign manner.

- Do you save indefinitely magazines that may have articles you really 'should' read because you might miss something?
- Do you need more than one 'repair drawer' or 'junk drawer'?
- Do you save things that seem just too good to throw away even though you have no particular plans for ever using them?
- Are you storing all sorts of things on behalf of your grown-up children?
- Do you save broken things for years, never repair them, and then realize you don't like or need them anyway?
- Do you lose your keys or wallet or purse regularly?
- Do you buy things you already have, but didn't know it because the cupboard is a rat's nest?
- Do you have under your kitchen sink cleaning products – including numerous 'miracle' cleaners – that you've never touched?

- Do you save spare parts to unknown things?
- Do you collect empty boxes?
- Do you know what bills will be due to be paid this week or this month?
- Have you lost a chunk of change because you're late with payments and suffer interest charges because there's no time to write the cheques?
- Has your collection of porcelain ducks, frogs, penguins, elephants, etc., begun to seem like it's just something else to clean – without the interest or fun that it once had?
- Are some drawers or shelves stuffed so full that you can use only the items on top?
- Do you keep putting things in places that you know aren't right and then tell yourself you are just putting them there 'for now'?
- Do you live in a house with more storage space than ever before, but every spare space fills up immediately and you still don't have enough?
- Do you feel guilty and depressed about the state of your home?
- Would you entertain more often (if at all) if you could only get things under control?

Aren't you glad that wasn't a test?

If you didn't feel that you had an interest in controlling clutter, it's doubtful you would have picked up and read this far. So let's move on to parts of this book that are more like answers than reminders of our lack of organizational success.

Here's how we've organized this book. First we propose a set of rules that can apply to all manner of households, regardless of their size, number of occupants, or magnitude of clutter.

After the rules, we explore some of the psychological roots of the clutter problem, because at heart it's a behavioural phenomenon. Insight into the dynamics of your cluttering behaviour may afford you great and tangible relief.

In the next and largest part of the book, we list specific, step-by-step solutions to clutter and organization problems. Not hints at solutions. Solutions. We call it 'Uncluttering Guides: An Alphabetical List'. For each topic we will tell you what items (if any) you'll need to implement a solution and how to proceed each step of the way until you've solved a specific clutter problem. But our approach is practical. It's usually how to do something, not what sort of organizing gadget to run out and buy. We want you to put your house on a diet, not stuff it into a girdle.

We're not suggesting that there are no alternatives. There are. But the solutions we offer have been tested by us or by others and found to solve specific clutter problems. We don't list four or five different solutions. We prefer to do the research, test the options, and then offer you the best solution available. We confess that this is just a touch authoritarian, but it's exactly the approach that will save you the most time.

In 'Uncluttering Guides', where you jump in is up to you. Topics are in alphabetical order. If you want to implement them all, just start at the beginning. Or rate them in order of what is driving you crazy the most and start there.

1   The Uncluttering Rules

Here are the rules that are your path out of a way of life bogged down with stuff, immobilized by disorganization, and stymied by interruption. They will assist you in your day-to-day decision-making process when clutter or household organization is the subject at hand. Keep these rules in on-going use even after you've uncluttered your life, so you'll keep it that way.

Rule 1   When in doubt, throw it out

Absolutely nothing else we say in this book can have such a liberating effect on your life.

There's an abundance of opportunities to acquire things in our lives. We are invited to do so by every imaginable source of advertisement; by our perpetual comparisons and our possessions with those of our friends, relatives, and neighbours; and by our own private insecurities and habits. We feel like we're building our nest. The more things we can add to our nest, the more secure and successful we feel.

Once an item makes it into our nest, a metamorphosis takes place as it becomes 'ours', and its value is completely transformed. For example, before a crystal decanter becomes our possession, if it should be broken or lost it would barely qualify as an accident. Once we get it into our home, however, if it is broken we regard it as a disaster. Obviously this has something to do with how much we paid for it, but it can acquire its own almost inexplicable value, which involves much more than money alone.

The trouble is, acquiring everything you have the chance to is just not worth it. The price paid is a lifetime of being loaded down by things we wouldn't miss if they were taken away from us: things we couldn't find if we needed them, things we don't even remember we have unless we see them, unused things that ultimately crowd out the necessary things we actually use. Don't wait for that to happen – do it of your own free will now.

The Cost of Storing Your Things

One major incentive to declutter is the expense of maintaining all that stuff. You'll be amazed when you figure out the actual cost of keeping it. First calculate how much you're paying for each square foot of your home by dividing the square footage by the mortgage or monthly rent you pay or what you could let it for. For example, if you live in a 1,000 square-foot house and have a £1,000 monthly payment, that's obviously £1 per square foot per month. Now multiply by how many square feet are devoted to storage. This can be an eye-opening experience. Let's say you've let an entire room slowly drift into a 'junk' room even though it was originally intended as a guest bedroom or a sewing room. You've got 100 square feet or more devoted to storage in that one room alone. So you're paying 100 X £1 = £100 a month for the privilege of having a junk room. That might be worth it if you were storing prized and valuable possessions.

Unfortunately, this monthly £100 bill is for storing items you don't even look at – unless you take a peek when you open the door to toss something else in the collection. Worse yet, just knowing what lurks behind that door nags you silently. You also have a crisis if you do have a guest. And your sewing plans are on indefinite hold – like perhaps for this lifetime.

A 'junk' room is only the most obvious place to look. For many homes, it's just the tip of the iceberg. Consider some of the other fertile places around the house to discover caches of junk. And add their cost to the first figure you came up with. For example:

· How many square feet of each cupboard in your home are used to store things you don't use? It's not nice to remind you of all the clothes in those wardrobes that no longer fit. Let's just say they're too large, shall we, and leave it at that. Or maybe you don't wear them because they've gone out of style. With luck, they'll come back in style in thirty years, but do you think you'll actually wear those musty antiques?

· What about under the beds? Gifts you've received that you're never going to use. Perfectly fine other things that are 'too good to throw away'. Broken things.

· Look in drawers, but don't count the things you use every day – or even once a year. What about the linen from your grandmother for a table that wouldn't even fit into your dining room? Linen with spots, linen with holes, linen you're saving for your kids. (They don't even like the brand-new things you get them for their birthday and Christmas. Lord knows what they'll want with things you don't even know what to do with.) And then there are the drawers bursting with unused blouses, shirts, socks, underwear, incomplete bed sheet sets, worn-out towels, photographs, calendars, school or university papers, postcards, ancient mail, maps, newspapers, and mystery items.

· Bookshelves filled with books you haven't looked at in years – if ever. Or with porcelain frogs. Or with decanters. We're not opposed to collections *per se*; it's just that it's sometimes difficult to appreciate the beauty of a porcelain frog if there are thirty-seven of them.

- Don't forget books that are stored in places other than bookshelves, including unloved cookery-books, outgrown children's books, and unused reference books.
- Appliances and gadgets you never use. They're often in the kitchen drawers and cabinets, but don't forget the extra set of speakers or the foot massager, no matter where you have stored them.
- The freezer. You have things in there that no one in the house knows about or can identify anymore – let alone would be willing to eat.
- The garage, carport, basement, or loft – junk heaven. Tyres for cars you no longer own. Athletic equipment such as the exercise bike that started in the living room, migrated to the bedroom, and is now relegated to dusty solitude. Dead clothes that no longer fit in your bulging wardrobes. Bed parts. Derelict lawn furniture or equipment. Pieces of wood left over from a project half completed in 1976. If by chance you can no longer fit your car or cars into your garage or carport, don't forget to add the additional depreciation caused by storing it outside. And add the square footage of the garage to your total storage bill.

The point: You have junk stored in many places in your home, and it costs you real money to store it.

Here are some guidelines for deciding what should be

thrown out and what should be kept. (When we say 'thrown out', we are including giving it away or selling it, of course.)

Popular Excuses for Keeping Things Forever

If you aren't actually using something, why allow it to complicate your home? I have a section of my desk drawer that is reserved just for pens. It's always overflowing. The problem is, if my favourite pen isn't there, I will turn the house upside down looking for it rather than use any of the pens that are stuffed into this drawer. Solution? Save the favourite pen plus three or four spares and discard the rest. Now there's room for adding something to the drawer should the occasion arise. And the drawer even closes easily, for the first time in years. If you have several pairs of spectacles with outdated prescriptions, give them away. (Several charities solicit them.) It's different if you use something occasionally. (Christmas ornaments are a good example.)

Give your grown-up childrens' things back to them. If you do, maybe they'll learn to deal with clutter a couple of decades earlier than you did. The same goes for your friends, neighbours, or other relatives for whom you are storing things.

Please don't try the old excuse 'It's too nice to throw away.' Especially if it's so nice, give it to someone who will use it and appreciate it.

If it's broken, fix it or throw it out. If it's torn, have it mended. If it doesn't fit, have it altered. don't put it anywhere just 'for now' and keep it in a perpetual holding pattern.

If you find a screw or have one left over after a project, don't start saving them. It will drive you crazy. Usually when you buy something that needs a screw, it will have one included. If it doesn't, you can get the exact number of appropriate screws while you're at the shop. That's much faster and easier than picking through all your saved screws (which over time have a way of starting to get nails mixed in with them, plus a few tacks, drawing-pins, washers, picture hangers, and other small, sharp, and rusty objects). And even if you do search your collection and ultimately find three of the screws you need, the project will probably call for four of them.

Since most households do have need of a nail or a screw occasionally, just remember that almost any method of acquiring and storing them is preferable to the one-at-a-time-whenever-you-happen-upon-one method and then adding it to the little box or mayonnaise jar full of them.

Save the stereo box for thirty days. If the stereo hasn't broken by then, discard the box. (If you bought it by mail order, save it for the full warranty period.) Unless you're planning on moving (have the date set, etc.), don't keep the box 'because you'll need it when you move.' That's true, but it may be years away. You or the moving company can use another box when the time comes.

Rule 1 still counts if you don't know what an item is. My mother will save something even though she's not at all sure what it is. She'll convince herself that it fell out of her refrigerator or something else vital and that if she throws it away, she will only then discover where it should have gone. If she weren't my mother, I would point out to her that she has lived for over sixty years. If she hasn't learned what something is by now, there is no particular likelihood she will do so in the next sixty years.

Rule 2   Use it or lose it

This rule is particularly helpful when you are attempting to implement Rule 1 and are getting rid of some of your stuff. How do you decide what to keep and what to discard? Sensible advice for this rule is if you're not using something, get rid of it. This does not allow you to plan on using it tomorrow. How does the song go? *'Mañana* never comes.'

Future time is especially not a factor in this rule. 'Use it' refers to the here and now. It doesn't mean some time in the future. You don't have to use something every day, but you can't use the excuse that it 'might come in handy after the earthquake' – unless it's a torch or something sensible. Not your collection of lampshades. If you haven't made any strawberry jam since 1986, despite your strong conviction that you will do so again next year, you can safely give away your jars and lids.

There is a twist to applying this rule that's very helpful to parents trying to teach children about clutter. You might phrase the rule: 'Put it away or lose it.' We received a letter from a woman who told us how well this version of the rule worked for her. She cleaned every Saturday morning and just threw out anything left in her way! It didn't matter if it was clothes, toys, or food. Out it went. No bluffing. A particularly brief period of time elapsed before the house was *completely* free of debris by early Saturday morning. Hard to argue with success.

Always remember that if you reduce clutter, you make house-cleaning that much easier.

Rule 3   Efficiency counts, so store things accordingly

Perhaps you've seen the classic film *Cheaper by the Dozen*. The head of the household in this film was an efficiency expert. (Remember them? Businesses used to hire them all the time. They still do, but they call them management consultants now.) This particular efficiency expert devoted his life to the study of such things. He found, for example, that it was considerably faster to button his shirt starting at the top and buttoning downwards compared to starting at the bottom and buttoning upwards. This little gem of knowledge in itself may not reduce clutter, but efficiency boils down to a maximum of output with a minimum of input, and it's a concept that's crucial to managing clutter.

Efficient storage reduces clutter by making it easier to replace things after each use. If it's easier it's more likely to happen. Efficient storage means that what you need is close to where you use it or where you expect it to be. Move things so they are efficiently placed for use and replacement. For example, if the recycling bins are in the far end of the garage, no one is going to use them. In the kitchen, move the silverware and plates to a drawer and cupboard between the table and the dishwasher. Put the glasses between the sink and the dishwasher. Since the children normally throw their coats just inside the door (if you're lucky), move the coat rack there, even though it looks better next to the desk down the hall. It's not carved in stone that you must store the vacuum cleaner in the upstairs cupboard. Move it downstairs, where it's more convenient. If your excuse is that there is no room in the downstairs cupboard, see the section on how to clean it out, get it organized, and create the room you need (page 73).

Efficient storage also means that things you use most often are stored in the most easily accessible places. In other words, 'hot' items go in 'hot' places. You'll have your own list of 'hot' items, of course, but it'll probably include things such as measuring spoons and cups, keys, bottles of spray cleaners, the roll of Sellotape, the corkscrew, the good pair of scissors, the dishwasher powder, etc. Resist the temptation to return rarely used items to a 'hot' (and therefore convenient) spot. If you're not alert, the anchovy paste will end up in front of the mustard. The silver polish will get shoved in front of the soap powder. Or the wood bleach will block your access to the furniture polish. 'Hot' places are easily reachable ones such as top drawers, eye-level cupboard shelves, and the front sections of shelves.

Store all similar things together – such as all the different sizes and shapes of flower vases you own. When you need one, you only have to look in one place. Also, you'll have no decision to make after you clean a vase and wonder where to put it. The same applies to food inside the cupboards and even inside the fridge. The easier you make it for things to get put where they belong, the less clutter will appear. You'll also have a fighting chance of finding what you're looking for if it's where it belongs. That can be a surprisingly gratifying experience.

Rule 4   Handle some things once

This rule is necessary because of the excuse 'for now'. For example, 'I will put this jacket here for now,' or 'I will put this stack of papers here for now.' This phrase should be forbidden to a known clutterer.

Once you say 'for now', you are admitting that you are

going to handle whatever it is more than once. That seemingly innocuous decision increases clutter and at least doubles your work-load. What you're really doing when you utter those forbidden words is putting off making a decision about it right then and there. Don't be lazy. That decision won't go away just because you put it off, and it won't be any easier to make later on. So make your decisions about things right then and there.

Here's one way to apply this rule: When the post arrives, don't just idly sort through it looking for something interesting. Instead, stand next to a wastepaper basket as you sort. Get rid of the appropriate pieces then and there. It's a very liberating thing to do. Put bills in the 'bills' file of your filing cabinet (see Rule 7). Put interesting catalogues or ads with the newspaper and look at them after you read the paper. Then file them as needed or recycle them with the newspaper.

We met a woman who stood at the dustbin as her children brought home paperwork from school. She looked at each paper, made the appropriate comments directly to her children, and threw it in the dustbin. If the paper was special in some way and merited saving, she had a place for it in her filing cabinet.

My mother's repair drawer was a great example of the lengths to which the 'for now' philosophy could be carried. Putting something in that drawer was exactly the same as throwing it away, because *nothing* ever emerged from it. We just kept more and bigger repair drawers to hold all that stuff.

When the opportunity arises, or whenever you feel the words 'for now' starting to form on your lips, remind yourself to handle the item once. Don't leave it in some temporary holding area instead of where it ultimately belongs.

Rule 5   Recycle it

We're not talking about just paper, aluminium, glass, and plastic. You may argue that you throw these items away anyway, so how does recycling help with uncluttering? Well, for one thing, it's a good habit to get used to putting certain things in certain places. In addition, many people have a tough time parting with containers, especially glass bottles. Mayonnaise jars are good for storing bacon fat, and pickle jars or jam jars are just right for something else. Recycling finally allows the world's bottle-savers to put their bottles to good use. Recycle them. The same goes for plastic ice-cream containers, with their irresistible resealing lid, and microwave plates that remain after the dinner has been eaten. Even if you can't recycle plastic in your area, don't save these disposable items.

Other things can be recycled also. What about clothes you no longer wear or fit into? Recycle them into the hands of someone who needs them. Don't forget old sweaters and shoes that aren't so obvious when you open the wardrobe door. What about books that overflow the capacity of your bookshelves? Sell them to a second-hand bookseller, or give them to a school library. Magazines can be given to a school or hospital or nursing home full of folks who will enjoy them. If you don't want to go to the trouble of finding a new home for your old magazines, recycle them with your newspapers if allowed. Old towels can be used for rags only if you need more rags. Otherwise, recycle them along with your old clothes. The same goes for unused linen, baby clothes, nappies, ties, belts, handbags, wallets, plants, or bikes. In fact, almost any inanimate object in your house is a candidate for reuse by someone else.

Rule 6   Pick a number and stick with it

If you really do use an empty mayonnaise jar for storing fat go ahead and save one. But if you use one mayonnaise jar every six months for fat, and you purchase mayonnaise approximately once a month for consumption, you only need to save one jar to have a sufficient supply. One. *Uno.* One more than zero. Don't save any more jars until you use the one you've saved.

If you intend to save boxes for packaging future gifts, pick a number and stick with it. If you're convinced that you must save a box for each of the different potential sizes of gifts, you really ought to call a spade a spade and just open a shop, because that's what you'll have with so many boxes. Limit your collection to four boxes of varying sizes stored inside the largest one. That should be all you'll ever need at any one time, or at least until you have a chance to replenish your supply. When you reach your number, don't save another box until you use one from your supply. If you do come across another irresistible box, then throw out one when you add the new one to your collection.

Whatever you do, don't exceed the chosen number. It's not fair to change the number willy-nilly. Pick a number for other things around the house that contribute to overall clutter. For example, decide to keep two weeks' worth of *Woman's Own* or *Hello!* Each week, throw away the issue that's three weeks old when the new one arrives.

If you have a passion for purchasing, this rule is for you. Handbags are prime examples. Once again, pick a sensible number of bags to keep, and stick with it. If you decide on seven, this means that the other bags are clutter. Rank your top seven handbags, give the others to charity, and don't buy a new one until you're willing to let one go.

Use this rule with shoes, socks, porcelain frogs, mustard jars in the fridge, or packages of paper towels in the cupboard. Also work clothes. Two sets are enough. Any more than that and you're just trying to get around giving away your old clothes. Junk drawer? Yes, you can keep it, but only one per household – not one per person or one per room.

Instead of a number, you can use a capacity if it's appropriate. For example, when you've accumulated more books than will fit into your bookshelves, it's time to get rid of some books.

Rule 7   Use a filing cabinet

Every contemporary home needs a filing cabinet – not just those with a home office or those belonging to your super-organized friends. Even if you don't have a desk – or instead of one if you don't have room – invest in a filing cabinet. You can always use the dining room table as a temporary desk, but nothing else in the house is a substitute for a filing cabinet.

Filing cabinets start at about £40 for a metal one with two drawers. An office-quality filing cabinet of the same size can be much more expensive. There are definite advantages to the more expensive ones: the drawers open fully so you can easily file all the way to the back. The drawers in the cheap ones don't open more than two-thirds of the way, so filing in the back of the drawer is always a pain. The more expensive ones have more reliable, stronger, and quieter opening and closing mechanisms. But even if you get the cheapest one available, it's still a great deal.

The two-drawer letter-size model is the right size for most homes. We will list some of the items to store in your cabinet below, which will help you decide if you need more than two drawers. You will find an Uncluttering Guide on page 91 on setting up your new filing system.

Some new cabinets have built-in metal frames for hanging file folders. If not, purchase an add-on frame for each drawer. And get a supply of the hanging files themselves. One of the reasons some people don't like filing cabinets is because they have never used them with hanging files. These hanging files are what changed the cabinet into the wonderful clutter-buster it is.

Besides being a perfect storage place for such obvious choices as bills, important papers, and correspondence, the filing cabinet is just right for warranty cards, product information, instruction booklets, stationery, photos, stamps, your children's important schoolwork reports, spare batteries, diskettes, pens, pencils, tax returns, receipts, invoices, telephone books and certain other books you want nearby, such as dictionaries, catalogues, address books, photo albums, and more. All sorts of nontraditional items can be stored in files, to your advantage.

Rule 8   Do something

This rule really isn't as glib as it sounds. We're encouraging you to proceed to action in order to solve or fix something that's bothering you. In the Introduction, we suggested that most of us have some idea of what to do to solve our own clutter problems. We may not know exactly what to do, or exactly where to start, or what to discard and what to save, or what we need to buy in the way of shelves or storage baskets. But we do know we need to clean out, discard, and organize. Unfortunately, for many of us, what we do best with our clutter is to fret about it and mull it over. We may practically salivate when we see a catalogue with a selection of products for getting organized or when we see a sale of cupboard organizers, but we're still stuck by our own indecision and inertia.

In fact, much of the thinking we do about clutter can lead directly to inaction. The more you think about something and become aware of the possible solutions, ramifications, and roadblocks to those solutions, the more you're racked with indecision and inaction.

Embrace your own little imperfections. Even if you live to be a hundred, you'll never be as organized as your friend John, but then again you'll never be as messy as your friend Deborah, either. Get the areas of clutter that bother you under control and stop beating yourself up over the rest. Even if what you do is unsuccessful, you'll feel better. Besides, it's quite unlikely your efforts will make the problem worse – particularly if you use these rules and the Uncluttering Guides that follow to solve specific headaches.

Rule 9 A place for everything and everything in its place

Obviously your parents thought of this rule before you did, but maybe that's just another reason why it's so important for getting rid of clutter. Some clutter is just stuff that belongs somewhere else. Whether it's the kids' toys strewn through the house, a wardrobe full of clothes that no one in the family wears any longer, newspapers piled in the corner, or paper stacked on the desk, these items are clutter as long as they're not in their proper place.

Clearly, it's must easier to decide to put everything in its place than it is actually to do it – especially if you've run out of places. Several of the earlier rules will help you reduce the number of things in your household. The Uncluttering Guides that follow will help you increase the number of places for all your things.

The other side of this rule means that if everything is in its place, you can find an item precisely when you want it. That event can sometimes make your day.

Rule 10 Items displayed in the house have to pass a test

This seems only fair. After all, you have only so much space. The items taking up that space should justify themselves. It's not a complicated test. They just have to have a valid reason for being there. The reason can involve function *or* form. For example, if the antique clock on the coffee table no longer works, it has lost its function. But it may still be quite beautiful to you and therefore has an attractive form. No problem. It passes the test. But it doesn't pass just because someone put it there 'for now' five years ago and it's never been moved since, or because someone who gave it to you might notice if it's gone, or because you don't know where else to put it.

The way to implement this rule is to walk through each room in your house and quickly test each item displayed on side tables, coffee tables, bedside tables, counters, mantelpieces, shelves, or anywhere else. Examine each item as you come to it. Ask questions such as: Why am I keeping it? What is it doing there? If it has a function, does it work? Am I sick and tired of dusting or cleaning it? Do I have others like it stored elsewhere? Then ask if you enjoy seeing it as you enter the room. How does this item really look sitting there for all the world to see or to use? Use your critical eye.

Don't rid your home of things you cherish. But you will likely discover that many of the knick-knacks, trinkets, and bric-à-brac sitting around your home fail the test. All the better. Anything that fails is one less thing to dust. Remove such items and deal with them accordingly: discard, sell, give away, or store elsewhere.

If you're not sure what to do with items that didn't

pass the test (such as the ash-trays made by one of your children), try putting them away in storage areas for a test period of one month. Your guilt is assuaged, and you've made progress in clutter control. Who knows what will happen in a month? We have an inkling you'll have forgotten about them completely – unless it's to remember, when you're cleaning, that you have fewer things to dust or wipe. When you clean out the drawers or cupboards they're temporarily stored in, you can make further decisions about them as needed.

Rule 11   Don't do things 'later'

Let's say you just spent an hour tidying up in the family room. It's in impeccable shape – splendidly uncluttered by things that don't belong there. You know only too well that it can be turned into a war zone by the family in minutes: discarded clothes, food, dirty dishes, shoes, toys (children's, dogs', and cats'), soft drinks and/or beer cans, dirty ash-trays, school papers, newspapers, magazines, cups, and glasses.

It goes something like this: One child comes into the family room with a cola and turns on the TV. He tosses his coat on a chair and rummages around for the TV guide. The desire for a sandwich becomes irresistible. He abandons the empty cola can and returns to the kitchen, gliding by both the rubbish bin where the cola can belongs as well as the coat hook where the jacket belongs. A few more trips by other family members and the room is done for.

Things Not to do Later: A Partial List

1 If you brought stuff into a room, take it back out *the very next time you leave that room* (after you're done with it, of course).
2 Take things upstairs if you are going there anyway.
3 Take things downstairs if you are going there anyway.
4 Take everything out of the car that was added this trip.
5 Pick up things when they drop.
6 Wipe up spills when they happen.
7 Vacuum up messes when they occur.
8 Wash dirty dishes and wipe off the counters before the food dries on them.
9 Fold the clothes when they emerge from the tumble-dryer.
10 Iron clothes while they're still slightly damp.

A lot of the clutter in your home will disappear if you follow this rule. It's not much more than leaving a room the way you found it. If there wasn't toothpaste spread on the sink before you came into the room, there shouldn't be any there when you leave it. This rule solves clutter problems without adding one second of time or one ounce of work to anyone's overwhelmed schedule. It doesn't involve any extra time to take dirty dishes to the sink if you're going there anyway to get a glass of water. It doesn't take any extra time to carry your shoes to your bedroom if you're going up there anyway to do your homework.

In some cases it actually saves a lot of time. If you don't wipe up a spill when it happens, it will eventually take much more than a simple wipe. It may call for hard scrubbing or several different scrapers or cleaners that require a trip to the garage or the shop. It may even have developed into a permanent stain.

Naturally, you know and practise all these sterling principles. It's the other members of your family who are somewhat less enlightened. So how do you get them to co-operate? Setting an example sometimes works (every ice age or so).

But this rule isn't going to get off the ground unless everyone practises it, and consistently so. Try calling the household together and sitting down at a peace conference with them. Tell them the subject of the meeting, and all parties will probably readily agree (with varying degrees of enthusiasm, perhaps) that clutter is a problem. Ask everyone to volunteer ideas for your own 'things to do later' list. Don't allow accusations to be hurled. Just make the list. Read them our list if you need help getting started with yours. Next, make a contract, with your new list as its terms. All parties must affirm that they agree to the terms. Then agree on a list of rewards for adhering to the contract and punishments for infringing it. Nothing extravagant or gruesome. Just an appealing pay-off for compliance and a somewhat obnoxious deterrent for non-compliance.

There are several additional ideas for things to do daily that will help keep the house civilized between cleanings, save time when you do clean, and contribute to your sense of successfully managing your home.

In the bathroom: Put a window squeegee (or a squeegee specially designed for the bathroom) in your shower. The last person to shower should use the squeegee to remove water from the walls and doors that would otherwise dry and turn into difficult-to-remove water spots. It only takes a minute or so. Not only will this make cleaning the shower easier than it's ever been before, the shower also will continue to look clean for a much longer time. If you have particularly hard water in your area, take one more step and quickly wipe the walls dry with a towel after you've squeegeed them. Now, cleaning the shower every week or every other week practically drops off your list of things to do because it never really stays dirty. Do the same thing around the basin. The last user should mop up the water on the surrounds and then dry and shine the chrome. Dry the basin itself if hard water makes that difficult to clean later. Use a towel that's on its way to be laundered, or leave a special towel or cleaning cloth hanging nearby.

In the kitchen: Wipe the counter, worktop or table, sink,

and chrome dry after each meal. Also after preparing a meal, take a couple of dampened paper towels and wipe the floor – but only the small area of the floor close to where you prepared the food – and in front of the refrigerator, if it needs it.

*For the rest of the house:*Vacuum as often as daily when pet hairs or general debris are getting to you. We're not suggesting a full-blown vacuuming, just a quick vacuuming of the main traffic areas for three or four minutes. To make this even faster, leave your vacuum in the corner of the dining room (or somewhere else, but not put away) during those times of the year that require frequent vacuuming. Besides making the house look so much better, this extra vacuuming also saves time when you do your regular cleaning. Your carpets and floors will look better longer and last longer.

Rule 12   Label things

We're not talking about putting a label just on the kids' gym shorts, although that's a prudent idea. We're talking about labelling things around the house –things that people don't label because they don't think of it or because they think it isn't necessary. How often have you gone to a storage cupboard to retrieve something from a cardboard box you had stored there yourself, only to find that there are now six cardboard boxes there and they all look the same? You start by getting down what you think is the correct box and taking off the tape with which you so carefully sealed it. After you discover that the item isn't in that box, you halfway reseal it with the used tape and start in on the next box. Let's say you do eventually find the item you're looking for – it's just that it's forty-five minutes and six boxes later. That's the kind of problem that labelling can avoid.

Label Storage Boxes

Label *all* storage boxes to avoid the grief outlined above. Get a good marking pen and, at least on cardboard boxes, write on the box itself. Try hard to avoid the label 'Miscellaneous'. Other examples of labels that may come back to haunt you are 'Garage Sale' or 'Charity'. Even if your label ends up listing everything in the box, doing so is still simpler than looking through your entire collection of boxes. Usually you can get away with a label such as 'Books' or 'Summer Clothes' – as long as you don't have more than one box with that same label. Use a label just complete enough so you can tell what's in the box without actually opening it. When you add or remove items from a box, change the label accordingly.

Label Frozen Food

Everything starts to look alike after a few days in the

freezer. That's understandable if you wrap items in aluminium foil, of course, but food stored even in cling film turns white and crystalline and becomes disguised quickly enough.

Put a roll of inch-wide masking tape and a pen in a drawer next to the cling film or foil. Use a length of the tape to make a label for everything you freeze. Also add the date to the label: if you have more than one package of chicken, you'll know which one to use first. As long as you have your tape handy, you might as well date even prepackaged frozen food so you'll know what to use first, what to save, and what to throw out when you defrost the freezer.

Label Cupboards Sometimes

Labels on the inside of cupboard doors can help keep your cupboards from disintegrating into chaos about as fast as you can get them organized. Even with the best of intentions, when you or others in the household bring home the groceries and unload them into the cupboards, you can't exactly remember where you decided to put certain items. Putting labels on the inside of the cupboard doors will help prevent haphazard storage. You may need labels just until you and the family get used to putting certain things in certain places. But even if labels become a permanent installation, they can keep a major reorganization effort intact.

With small children you can put the labels on the outside of the cupboards – especially the ones they tend to get into while looking for cereals, sugar, biscuits, jam, honey, bread, etc. Lord knows it's not that they need to know where these things are. Rather, it's a reminder of where to replace things when the users are finished with them. If they're too young for verbal labels, use pictures instead.

Speaking of your wonderful progeny, use labels generously in their rooms to teach them to put things where they belong. In the Uncluttering Guides that follow, see 'Children's Rooms', on page 71 for more ideas.

2 The Psychology of Clutter

The landscape of your house matches the inner land-scape of your thoughts and feelings. In other words, we can gain some insight into its nature by examining it from a psychological point of view. In all but the rarest of cases, it's not a medical problem. And (we hope) the need to clutter isn't programmed into us genetically. Chimpanzees make nests to sleep in, but they walk away from them after each use. And they do not have charming collections of coconuts, bugs, leaves, etc.

Just because it has psychological dimensions does not mean that anyone living amid a patch or two of clutter has a psychological problem. Were that true, we'd all be on the couch.

When Has Clutter Become Clutteritis?

At what point can we say that clutter has gone beyond the point of reasonableness? Where is the psychological boundary between a reasonable amount of clutter and a more persistent problem?

In our view, clutter becomes a problem that calls for action when one or more of the following situations arise for you or for other members of the household:

· It is creating feelings of depression, anxiety, or desperation.
· The need for more or better or newer stuff seems insatiable.
· You feel like you are not the master of your own life any more: it feels as if you're being controlled by your possessions.
· The disorder of your living space prevents you from feeling comfortable or creative or happy when you're there.
· You deride yourself for not being more organized.
· You're in chronic conflict with other household members over this issue.
· You're ashamed to have friends and relatives over to the house because it's such a mess, and you're feeling more and more isolated or eccentric as a result.

Those are some of the psychological landmarks indicating that clutter has passed beyond the point where it can be ignored – at least if you want to promote a happy and productive life. Now let's dig into some of the psychological needs that feed the clutter habit.

Too Much Stuff: Pack Rats

A survey estimated that at least 10 per cent of Americans are chronic hoarders and there is no reason to suppose the percentage is different in the UK or other developed countries. The most common excuses given by the hoarders interviewed were:

1 'I might need it someday.'
2 'They don't make them like this any more.'
3 'It reminds me of someone I love or some place I've been.'

Familiar? We would like to propose the following rebuttals for each of these rationalizations:

1 Yes, you might need it some day. Then again, you might not. Assess the odds dispassionately. What will happen if you don't have the item on that imaginary day? Will you die? Will you be sick? Or will it just be an inconvenience that can be easily remedied? And are you going to save everything that you *might* need? If so, you'd have to live in a warehouse.
2 No, they probably don't make it like this any more. But you can admire something without concluding that you have to own it. If you save everything that fits in this category, you'll need a second warehouse.
3 Yes, these things remind you of people and places. But they are only that – reminders. They are not the

person or place in itself. The reality of the experience is still alive in you by virtue of the fact that you were forever changed by it. You are not betraying this person if you pass on an object that reminds you of him or her. (Can you imagine that person expecting you to be the object's custodian forever? What kind of friend is that?) If you fuss over the object, your affection can get displaced and fantasized so that it focuses more on the object than the real human being it calls to mind. If you were to save a token of every meaningful experience, you'd better start looking for a third warehouse.

Of course, no one is proposing that you become completely unsentimental or ruthlessly Spartan. We are talking about motives that can run amok if they're linked to objects that serve as symbols of security or attachments. The real roots of security and affection are within you.

The alternative is moderation. Take the middle path. Keep things that are genuinely important for your well-being. And keep things that you genuinely appreciate without feeling desperate or driven about keeping. And keep sentimental remembrances with a sense of joy, not obligation or guilt.

'This Is Me': The Roots of Clutter

The times in which we live will probably not be recorded as one of the great introspective or spiritual ages.

Unfortunately, the odds are on materialism – at least in the short term. Has any generation ever before had the abundance of material goods available to someone growing up in the West today? School-leavers have their hopes set on a new BMW – not the beaten-up Ford their parents longed for at their age.

What can account for such a phenomenal rise in the esteem of material goods? Look no further than the sense of self, and the remarkable human ability to see the self represented or symbolized in objects. 'See this collection of goodies? This is me – this is who I am. I am one great person, as you can see.'

So what's wrong with seeing oneself in an object? Doesn't everybody do it? Well, yes, they do. It is a supremely easy habit to fall into. But it has its problems. For one thing, at face value it is untrue. Our essence is not embodied in things. For another, the habit can lead to a frightful amount of offence being taken. 'How dare you insult my collection of penguins! I won't ever speak to you again!' And we put our sense of self-esteem out there on the line when we trot out our objects. If they are praised, we puff up and feel better. When they are scorned, we feel worse about ourselves. This can be quite a roller-coaster ride.

How do you get off the roller-coaster? Don't cling to a fixed view of yourself – especially one that needs objects to keep it afloat. You're entitled to exist just as you are, without an array of psychological props through which you define yourself.

Look at the penniless ascetics of the world's ancient cultures. They have little more than a begging bowl and a sheet, and yet they can be radiant human beings. Here's a poem by the Japanese haiku poet Basho that says a lot in five lines:

> *My house*
> *Burnt down*
>
> *I own*
> *A better view*
>
> *Of the rising moon.*

There is also the story of the monk who used to burn his house down every few years to make sure he was not getting attached to material things. We are not advocating such strong measures; the much more moderate ones in this book will do just fine.

At some level of awareness, you become the caretaker for every scrap of stuff you keep. Don't delude yourself. You are devoting a proportional amount of psychological energy to every object in your domain, whether or not you are aware of it from moment to moment.

Clutter as Tangible Procrastination

In a sense, clutter is the end result of procrastination – especially if your problem is not so much that you have too much stuff, but rather that the stuff you have is disorganized. You know all the anthems of the procrastinator: 'I'll start tomorrow', 'I need shelves before I can do anything', or even just 'I'll do it later'.

Clutter arises in a series of moment-by-moment decisions to postpone action. Consider yourself pouring a bowl of cereal. You pour the cereal in the bowl, perhaps spilling a flake or two in the process. Ditto for a drop or two of milk. Something good is on TV, so you head for the couch – leaving behind the open cereal box and milk carton, plus the crumbs and spilled milk. Thus ariseth clutter.

What went on there? At the precise moment that you had a choice about whether to leave a mess, you chose to rush into the next moment. The couch was waiting. You chose the next experience over finishing the one you started. You didn't allow yourself to feel the small satisfaction of closing the lid on the cereal and putting the rest of the stuff away. One more sticky little glob of psychic baggage was added to your unconscious. Coagulate a bunch of these globs together and you will have a messy, cluttered, disorganized home environment.

The alternative to this rush to the next sensation is to savour what's right in front of you. There's a little pulse of satisfaction, contentment, or even beauty in completing what you've started. Learn to fine-tune your antenna that picks up this bit of quiet pleasure, appreciate it, and cultivate it. True, it may be a subtle pleasure – as subtle as the burden each item of clutter added to your life – but if you encourage that pleasure, order will emerge effort-lessly.

To the anticipated chorus of excuses that procrastinators offer when action seems imminent, I offer this bit of graffiti that someone etched into wet cement on a San Francisco pavement: 'SHUT UP AND DEAL WITH IT'. It may not be the most polite bit of advice, but it has a wonderful ring of usefulness about it.

The Slobs vs. the Fuss-pots

There have been struggles between peoples since time immemorial but they pale in comparison to the struggle taking place under the roofs of most households every day. We are talking about the slobs vs. the fuss-pots.

We're not sure if everyone in the world fits into one of these two categories, but it seems as if most are certainly inclined one way or the other. Perhaps you are a slob trying to reform or a fuss-pot trying to learn a few new tricks. Either way, you are probably not pleased with the unpleasantness of arguing with the other half of the world.

It can get ugly. There you are, having spent all day Saturday cleaning the house. It is gleaming. Your significant other arrives home from a triumphant tennis match and drops his or her sweaty clothes on the floor, within reach of the laundry basket designed specifically to receive said garments. What are both of these people thinking? Probably something like:

YOU: You don't even realize I just cleaned the house. What a slob. You did this just to torture me.

SIG. OTHER: Great tennis game. Too bad I had to cheat. I can't wait to get in the shower.

The conversation (if there is one) runs something like this:

YOU: HU-neeeeee! I just cleaned the house, and look at what you're doing!

SIG. OTHER: Huh? Oh, yeah. Looks great. Are there any clean towels?

Not the most satisfying of scenes, is it? So what do you do if you live with a clutterer who is driving you crazy? He or she can tear the kitchen apart to open a tin of beans, will leave the mess behind, and will remain blissfully unaware of any problem. Or what if you live with a fuss-pot who is needling you incessantly? He or she wants the tea-towel folded every time it's hung up, or doesn't let the newspaper sit on the floor for ten seconds, or starts to wash the dishes before everyone's finished eating dinner.

First, let's try to lay out the reasoning from each point of view. We are calling each end of this axis by a slightly pejorative term (get over it) to keep it a fair fight: That's exactly how each one views the opposition. The fuss-pot perceives acts of sloppiness as deliberate acts – ones carried out spitefully to provoke, to retaliate against, or to torture the fuss-pot. The slob perceives acts of tidiness and organization as deliberate attempts to demean, to control, and to reform the slob.

From both points of view, a common theme is that the other's behaviour is viewed as highly personal – that is, it appears to be directed specifically at the perceiver. In our saner moments, of course, we know that isn't true. The slob is actually thinking about his or her mean boss, or yesterday's golf game, or tonight's dinner. The fuss-pot is really concerned with order or hygiene or cleanliness.

So the first step in dealing with this sort of conflict is to depersonalize it as much as possible. To the extent that you do, you will be able to avoid getting angry. These are events that are happening; in the vast majority of cases, they are not messages beamed directly at your sense of worth as a person. If you are very reflective, you'll notice that there's a split second between when you become aware of something that usually makes you angry and the actual emotional response of anger. In that split second, try to focus on the impersonal nature of the slob's or fuss-pot's behaviour. Does he or she really have you in mind? Is the person being deliberately malicious? Quite probably not. Keep your attention riveted on that fact, and you'll find that a lot of the emotional steam is taken out of these confrontations. Your friend is probably focusing on his or her own dear self, as is most of the world at any given moment.

Everyone is in the middle of his or her own truth. That of the slob, to the slob, is just as valid as the fuss-pot's truth. No sense in trying to mess with that. Might as well try asking a tornado to rotate the other way.

What you might have more success with, however, is a dialogue. Leave the words 'should' and 'ought' behind. They are control-oriented words that ooze rebuke between the lines. Accordingly, they are remarkably unsuccessful as agents of persuasion. You'll have better luck with expression. As the psychologist Albert Ellis has pointed out, 'prefer' is a much more workable term. *Tell* the other person how *you* are feeling and what *you* are thinking – not what you are convinced *they* are feeling or thinking. And *ask* the other person what's going on with him or her. Most slobs are sincerely surprised to find that fuss-pots are upset by a half-inch puddle of water in the middle of the bathroom. Most fuss-pots think everybody wants ironed underwear.

Humans being the odd creatures we are, if your partner became too similar to you you'd probably squabble even more. Don't try to make the other person into another version of you. It won't work. If you're compassionate and patient, what can emerge is an agreement to move toward each other's way of life at least a little bit, with as much respect and understanding as you can muster. This aiming toward the other person is the important thing, not whether you completely change your ways. If you can pick up the waterlogged towels you've thrown on the bathroom floor, maybe your partner can relax the dishwashing schedule just a bit. And *thank* each other along the way, even if it doesn't come naturally.

What if this idealistic programme meets with no success whatsoever? Well, the least you can hope for is to enable the other person to experience directly the consequences of his or her actions. If the slob leaves a trail of clothes all over the house, do you really expect any change if you follow along and pick up after him or her? Things are working out pretty well from the slob's point of view. Why put a perfectly good valet out of commission? But what would happen if the slob's clothes were regularly rounded up and deposited in a bin and left there? Maybe the owner would notice a drastic lack of apparel after a while – at least unrumpled apparel. Until slobs actually feel the consequences of their behaviour, there is little chance of success. The same is true for fuss-pots. If your favourite fuss-pot is spending all his or her spare time ironing doilies, maybe it would help to point out gently that a picnic is being planned and his or her company would be greatly appreciated.

Action Steps

Here are a few specific suggestions based on behavioural ideas that you might find helpful in dealing with your clutter habit:

· If you are embarrassed to invite others over because
the house is in such a mess all the time, as an antidote
go ahead and invite people over regularly. Start with
once a month, if that helps. It'll be a nudge to get you
to clean up your act. Do it often enough, and you'll
probably get used to an uncluttered house. So invite
someone over for tea or dinner. But make sure to
rotate guests, because a regular visitor will get used to
your mess.

· Your clutter wasn't accumulated in a day, so don't
expect it to be resolved in a day. Start with whatever
is bothering you the most. Appreciate the progress
you make along the way. Setting perfectionist goals
will just lead you into cycles of resolution and failed
attempts. Accept your less-than-perfect success (and
less-than-perfect self!).

· Don't declare 'I *am* a collector' any more than you
would say 'You *are* a bad child.' It creates a similar
sort of wound. It is not your essence to be a collector.
It is what you are doing at the moment – not what you
are being. If you define yourself as a collector or a
junkaholic, it will be that much more difficult to
change. You have defined yourself – not described
what you are doing, which is a much less loaded
question. What you are doing is far easier to change
than your view of yourself.

· Don't throw out a young child's favourite toy (e.g. a

teddy bear) without discussing it with the child. A teddy bear is a first-love object, and the child could be learning that loved ones can vanish in a rather drastic manner. If a rigid organizational system is imposed in too authoritarian a manner, paradoxically you may end up teaching a child to be a revenge clutterer.

· Remember that your child is modelling your behaviour. The wife of an acquaintance of mine was said never to have thrown away a single issue of any magazine that ever entered the house. One room of the house was devoted almost entirely to huge stacks of magazines that were going to be read 'some day'. She rinsed out and reused paper towels and aluminium foil. Was it therefore a surprise that her child refused to let go of a single toy, even if it was worn to shreds? When asked to throw away or give away a toy, he would scream 'IT'S MINE IT'S MINE IT'S MINE' at ear-splitting levels.

· Do you get stuck in the middle of a huge ambivalence when you're trying to decide whether to throw something out? When you're spending a great deal of time teetering back and forth, it seems like this is a very big decision. In truth, if you're spending that much time, it more likely means that there would not be a whole lot of difference in your life if the object stayed or if it didn't. Let it go.

· See how you feel when a room is clutter-free. Sit down in it and percolate awhile. Are you as happy as a sand-boy? Or do you feel mildly uncomfortable? If the latter, the clutter will return in short order precisely because you want it to. Stay with this feeling awhile and see if you can see yourself in a clutter-free room and enjoying it. Reflect on the fact that you are entitled to an orderly, beautiful environment no less or no more than anyone else.

· Are there parts of your life that you have successfully organized, especially at the office? Reflect on the skills you already learned in that domain. See if you can shift your opinion of your organizational skills accordingly: you're not a total slob after all! And then apply some of those skills to your home environment.

· Make an appointment with yourself – and then keep it – to spend a fixed and reasonable amount of time decluttering: a serious, write-it-down-in-your-book, don't-miss-it-unless-you're-sick-in-bed kind of appointment. It's the same kind of appointment you would routinely make with a doctor or with an important client at work.

3 Uncluttering Guides: An Alphabetical List

Sorry, but at this point you've run out of excuses: you've learned the rules. You've explored the psychology of clutter. It's time to get down and dirty.

Uncluttering is like putting your home on a diet, and the Uncluttering Guides that follow are the recipes to use to do just that. Like food recipes, they list all the ingredients and procedures you'll need to make the job as clear and painless as possible.

As mentioned before, either start with the area of clutter that's bothering you the most, or at the beginning of the alphabetical list, and work your way through it. Clutter will disappear from the house as it disappears from the list of things that are nagging at you and driving you crazy. The 'new' you will emerge – clutter-free, organized, and perhaps just the tiniest bit smug.

ANTI-CLUTTER EQUIPMENT

Products that will help you unclutter

Cupboards

1 To help arrange cupboards so that you can see the items stored in the back of the shelves, install tiered shelves you can purchase or make yourself.

2 To make finding a particular spice easier, install shelves the height and depth of one spice container so each spice is visible. Arrange spices alphabetically. The best place to mount this special spice shelf is on the inside door of an eye-level cupboard. If the shelves inside the cupboard make this impossible, the inside of a pantry door may work if you're lucky enough to have a pantry. Otherwise, mount them on a kitchen wall close to the main food-preparation area. Another alternative is a lazy Susan (see number 4).

3 Similar shelves on the inside of other cupboard doors are handy. For example, a metal wire shelf on the inside of the cupboard door under the sink is great for storing the wet dishcloth and scourer plus dishwasher powder and washing-up liquid. It makes it so easy to use and

retrieve these items that maybe you'll store them here instead of leaving them out as clutter on the worktop or draining board.

4   A lazy Susan is the next best alternative for storing your spices if you don't have a place to install the shelves mentioned above. Place it at the front of a prime storage shelf. Get the biggest lazy Susan your shelf will accommodate; the one with several different levels is best. Use it just for spices; don't store the salt-and-pepper-pots or other everyday items here. If you reserve it only for spices, it will at least have a chance to stay organized. Be sure to raise the shelf above the lazy Susan to make enough room to place and remove items behind the lazy Susan without knocking half the spices off.

A lazy Susan is also handy in bathroom cupboards. Use it under the basin to store the overflow from the medicine cabinet – or for all the hundreds of different makeups, powders, ointments, salves, and unguents that one certain household member seems to need. Let that person use this lazy Susan exclusively.

Drawers

Plastic drawer-organizers are available. Use them to divide up the junk in the junk drawer so you can find the screwdriver from among all the rest of the stuff, for a change. Use them to keep the little pieces of your pastry kit from becoming buried at the back of the drawer, or to keep pens and pencils and everything else organized in a desk drawer. Larger types of drawer organizers can be used to divide the socks from the T-shirts in the wardrobe or chest drawer.

Showers

Get a hanging tray that loops over the shower head and holds soap, several bottles of shampoo, and a cloth. It will also provide a spot to hang a squeegee for wiping down the shower walls once a day, which will help prevent soap and hard-water build-up.

Wardrobes

1   Add a second pole under the existing one for a second layer of shirt- or jacket-length clothes. It requires little more than measuring and drawing where you want it to be, going to the hardware shop for the pole and brackets, and finding a drill and a screwdriver to install it.

2   Instead of a second pole, or in addition to it, put stackable vented plastic storage boxes or open basket drawers under your existing pole for extra storage of folded clothing, socks, and shoes.

3   Put up as many hooks as you have room for. They're

great for hanging clothes that aren't quite ready for the laundry, for pyjamas, your favourite belt, scarves, handbags, or bathrobe. Don't forget to do the same thing in the children's wardrobes.

4   Add a shelf if there is wasted storage space above the existing shelf in your wardrobe or cupboard. One more high shelf is great for Christmas decorations, winter clothes in the summer, and summer clothes in the winter. Adding shelves in a tall, skinny utility cupboard can add much more storage space. Install shelves above the height of the broom and mop you have stored there. Alternatively, install shelves from top to bottom, and store the broom and mop on hooks on the inside of the door.

General Storage

1   Tool boxes are good for the kids' art supplies, your own sewing, or other small items. The newer plastic ones are inexpensive and, when not used for heavy tools, will last indefinitely.

2   A small basket on the kitchen worktop is good for keeping the coupons you want to save. A tall basket in the cupboard for the dry cleaning helps with something that's hard to get together at the last minute. Careful, though: baskets seem addictive to some people, and they can quickly change from useful storage to clutter.

3   A small chest will often fit under the jacket-length clothes in the wardrobe and can be used to store just about anything.

BIRTHDAYS

No more belated cards!

Have trouble remembering friends' and relatives' birthdays? Do you leave yourself little reminder notes and then discover them too late? Wouldn't it be nice to have enough time to pick up a card or gift without making a special trip? The solution is relatively painless – at least far less painful than the repercussions of forgetting certain people's birthdays!

On New Year's Day, sit down with your address book or computerized address file. Take out your new diary for that year. Take a fat red pen or pencil in hand and write the name of every person you want to remember in the appropriate box (or line) in the diary. If the person is out of the country, you might want to record a warning for yourself a week or so ahead: 'Mail Uncle Rufus's BD card.' The same precaution applies if the person's birthday is early in the month and will be lurking out of sight on the next page of the diary.

Apply this simple technique, and your friends and relations will marvel at your memory. You'll know better, but don't let on.

CHILDREN'S ROOMS

Organizing the room so the children will be

Two schools of thought apply. The first one is by far the simpler. Control the clutter in the kids' rooms by closing the door and keeping it closed. Never go in the room. Never even look in the room. Deposit clean clothes and other necessities outside the door the same way food is deposited outside a prison cell. If you avoid even fleeting glimpses of these rooms, you may be able to enjoy at least the illusion that your home is organized and clutter-free. If you can't (or won't), let's get to work on the second school of thought.

Giving Them a Chance to Succeed

One genuine excuse children have for not hanging up their clothes is that they can't reach the rods in the wardrobes. Lower the rods to a height that allows them to be reached. Ditto for hooks to hang things on. Both of these items are usually easy to raise or lower. If the rod is difficult or inconvenient to move, leave it in place and install a new rod at a lower level. Both the brackets and the rod are quite inexpensive and are available at hardware shops. Raise them over the years as the kids grow.

In the meantime, use those higher areas for storage.

Get a nice big basket for their dirty clothes and an oversized wastepaper basket for rubbish. The bigger and the lower these baskets are, the better your odds are that they'll actually be used. You can also use plastic baskets for toys and games. Baskets can also be used for clean clothes if you don't have enough drawer space or if the kids can't reach the drawers. Inexpensive plastic tool boxes are great for things such as crayons, art supplies, and other collections of smaller toys or supplies.

Once you have installed the necessary boxes and baskets and have lowered the rods and hangers in the closet, label all these items according to their purpose. Use words or pictures, depending upon the age of the child. Also label shelves, drawers, and cupboards.

If you're short of space in the children's rooms, you might consider an investment in a bed with built-in drawers under the mattress. Or add-on drawers can be installed under conventional mattress frames.

Is it Worth the Struggle?

This sounds like a lot of work for you. Is it really worth the effort? Even after you do the organizing, the really hard part will be to teach the children actually to use all these organizational tools. Our opinion is yes, it's worth it. Children want to learn. Doing everything for them is far from beneficial. The competence you hope they'll have later in life as adults starts with learning and acquiring skills sooner or later. Sooner seems better.

CUPBOARDS, BASEMENTS, GARAGES AND ATTICS

How to clean them out step by step

This guide focuses on cupboards, but it works just as well on a larger scale for cleaning out the basement, garage, or attic. It's one of your best allies in the eventual victory over clutter.

Go ahead and feel sorry for yourself if you want to. Apparently few people like to do this except when they're depressed. You're not alone in your dread of the giant can of worms this job may open. However, the pay-off is great and the sense of accomplishment splendid, so please persevere.

Supplies

Four to seven medium or large cardboard boxes. The exact number will depend upon the amount of stuff – especially whatever will be leaving your house when you're finished with this job. (You may substitute large plastic sacks instead – especially if not having any boxes will be used as an excuse – but they're harder to throw things into.)

It's best to do this while home alone – in part because you're going to need a large area to work in, but mainly because some difficult decisions will have to be made. Don't invite any more angst by assembling a committee to vote on all the stuff you're going to review. The benevolent dictator approach is much preferred. (Veto rights for those affected are optional.) Start this job early in the day because it's time-consuming and you're undoubtedly going to be interrupted.

Getting started is probably the most difficult part of this job. You have an inkling of what faces you and what a big mess you'll find when you start exploring corners of the cupboard that haven't seen the light of day for years. Be brave. First just place the cardboard boxes outside the cupboard in a semicircle, if possible. You're going to use these boxes to sort the items you remove from the cupboard. Label the boxes with a marking pen as follows:

1	Rubbish	5	Return to Owner
2	Garage Sale or Charity	6	Repair
3	Belongs Elsewhere	7	Altering or Mending
4	Not Sure		

Notice that none of your choices includes a box labelled 'Move to the Attic or Garage'. Box 3 is for an item you find in the cupboard that belongs in the kitchen, for example. Don't use box 3 as a sleazy excuse to shuffle items elsewhere in your house.

The plan is to empty the cupboard completely. Remove most items one at a time, not in big armfuls, and as you remove each item, drop it in the appropriate box. Remove even the things that rightfully belong here. You'll replace them a bit later. (Resist the impulse to paint the cupboard after it's empty. You'll decide you've done enough and put all the stuff right back in.)

So, for example, as you take out clothes, you may come across the sweater that you looked great in – before one spaghetti meal stained it and cumulative spaghetti meals had their impact on you. With a light heart, put it into the box marked 'Rubbish' or 'Charity'. (See Rule 2: 'Use it or lose it.')

When you come to the overnight bag in search of which your son tore the house apart twice, drop it in box 3 – 'Belongs Elsewhere'. Later you can store it with the rest of the luggage. (See Rule 3: 'Efficiency counts, so store things accordingly.')

When you come to the unused, never-even-taken-out-of-the-box attachments to the vacuum cleaner that you traded in three years ago, put it in box 1 ('rubbish'). Let's be very clear at this point: There is *no doubt* about discarding attachments for which you no longer have a vacuum cleaner. This is an *easy* decision. Right?

When you ultimately find six handbags that exceed the number you picked according to Rule 6 ('Pick a number and stick with it'), you'll have to decide which ones to keep and which ones to throw away. But don't do that now. Just put them in box 4 and continue grabbing items one at a time from the cupboard.

When you come across a school text-book (circa 1976) that you still believe, albeit by habit, you will refer to someday, you can easily be thrown into a panic. How can you possibly decide what to do with such books right this second? After all, you've been saving them for years, and you can't undo that decision without lengthy deliberation. No problem. Just drop them into box 4 ('Not Sure') and proceed.

Items you've been saving because they need repair generally belong in box 1. Keep them only if you make a special box for them (box 6) and promise actually to take them to be repaired.

The same goes for clothes that need to be mended or altered. You can't continue to save them and use the excuse that you're waiting until you know someone who will do this work for you. No one knows this person. Instead, look in the Yellow Pages under 'Tailors' or 'Dressmakers' (not 'Alterations' or 'Mending'). Take a chance with one of the listings and make an appointment. Put those items in box 7. When that box is full and you realize how much it's going to cost to mend clothes you haven't missed, cancel your appointment and change the box label to 'Charity'.

In sorting through the cupboard, we are proposing that you make decisions for the rest of the family. When you run into someone else's stuff, don't put it in box 4 ('Not Sure') every time, or you'll defeat the whole process. The rest of the household may not have your same concern about reducing clutter or reclaiming storage area. Apply the rules for controlling clutter to their possessions exactly as you would to yours. One little warning: Years from now, you may be accused by your children of causing them permanent psychological damage when you threw away their train set, Mickey Mouse Club membership card, or picture of Paul McCartney. If you would like to be extremely fair, announce one or two weeks prior to your starting this job that you intend to get rid of all unused stuff, no matter who it belongs to. Promote this warning along with serene assurances that they may retrieve any wanted items before you start the job. Otherwise they forswear the right to complain after you've thrown out or given away something of theirs. As you well know, it's very unlikely that anyone is going to go excavating through the cupboard in the armistice period. But at least you'll have a free hand and peace of mind as you sort through and make decisions about their possessions.

It's clear that the hardest part of this job is discarding things. We won't be flippant about how difficult it is to make decisions to part with items that have fond memories associated with them or that otherwise seem truly valuable to you. Here are some guidelines to help your decision-making:

1 Some sentimental things can and should be saved. You're only human. However, there are limits. You're not

going to forget your own wedding even if you give away your wedding dress. And some sentimental items can be saved in a different form. For example, take a picture of yourself holding your school tennis racket for one last time (it hasn't touched a tennis ball in twenty-two years), and then let the racket go to someone who will use it.

2 If you don't make some hard decisions and get rid of many items, you'll have as much stuff when you finish cleaning the cupboard as when you started. It may end up in different parts of the house, but your overall clutter inventory will only be redistributed, not reduced. Not exactly a wildly successful job of cupboard cleaning.

3 When you find yourself coming to item after item that you don't want to part with for which you're willing to break a rule, remember why you started this project in the first place. The clutter has bothered you, is bothering you, and will continue to bother you. Believe us that you will not miss these items when they're gone. For ages you hadn't thought of many of the items you're rediscovering. Had you not been cleaning out the cupboard, you wouldn't be thinking about them now. And you're not going to think of them again tomorrow. Honest.

Put the items to go back into the cupboard on the floor next to the boxes. Once the cupboard is empty, but before you move the boxes or start to refill the cupboard, first turn your attention to box 4 ('Not Sure'). Don't put this box off until last. If you do, you may run out of patience for the hard decisions required for it. The temptation will be just to slide the box right back into the cupboard. Besides, you still have boxes 1 and 2 close at hand. Hopefully you'll feel so good from successfully parting with some stuff that you'll transfer most of the items from Not Sure box into the boxes leaving the house and starting a new life elsewhere.

The next step is to take the remaining boxes to their appropriate places. If the recipients of the Charity box or boxes will pick them up, telephone and arrange it. Otherwise, load them into your car *now* and deliver them. *Don't put the boxes in the garage.* That's too dangerous. Far too often, the boxes become permanent fixtures in that new location. Sooner or later someone will have to go through all this sorting again because no one will remember what's in the boxes, or someone will go through each box to see if he or she agrees with your decisions.

Take box 3 ('Belongs Elsewhere') and distribute those items where they belong. This step can have the somewhat disconcerting effect of causing an overflow elsewhere. No matter. You can tackle that area when you're ready.

Finally, put what's left back into the cupboard. The reason you save this step for last is because it is by far the easiest. But there are rules about how to replace these items. When replacing clothes, there are several levels of organization that will save you time dressing each morning. First, separate items for above the waist from those for below the waist. Within those categories, put like items together, such as skirts, trousers, jackets, shirts, and accessories. Hang suits with suits and dresses with dresses. Put hangers all in the same direction. Throw out your extra supply of hangers, or recycle them with a local thrift shop.

Many wardrobes already have an additional pole for hanging clothes at a second level. It's an easy project to add one, and there's room in almost all wardrobes to add a pole under the shirt or blouse section. Go to a timber yard or a DIY store after measuring the required length. Add-on poles are also sold ready-made.

Some cupboards are apt to look practically empty once you get them organized. The feeling of being able to find what you're looking for – let alone the luxury of a little extra space for a change – more than compensates for having your 'nest' a bit less full.

COLLECTIBLES

It's OK to 'uncollect' a collection

A Collection is Born

It's startling how some inanimate objects seem to reproduce as if they were the real thing instead of replicas. Over time, rather than a frog sitting peacefully (and alone) on your bookshelf, there are so many frogs of various sizes and shapes that you've got a 'collection' – even though you may never have intended to create one – and you are a 'collector' – even though you don't feel any different. All you did was buy one little porcelain frog at a curio shop while on holiday a few years ago.

It Grows and Grows and Grows

Later a friend or relative noticed the frog sitting on your bookshelf and decided on your Christmas gift then and there. You accepted the gift of a second frog (what else are you going to do?) and put the new frog next to the original. Now that there were two of them sitting side by side, it was twice as likely that other people would get you more frog gifts. As the number of frogs grew, the likelihood of getting more increased exponentially, and before long you have more frogs than a June pond – most of which aren't nearly as nice as the one really wonderful original that you selected yourself.

Once in place, this collection can't be ignored. For starters, after there are a certain number of them they may be the most striking feature of an entire room. Unfortunately, it will usually be in a way that has nothing whatever to do with your original design scheme. They also require dusting and cleaning – neither of which is all that quick, because each one must be picked up and replaced to do so. They have truly become clutter in one of its more straightforward forms.

Have a garage sale, or give the entire collection to a charity or nursing or convalescent home. Or you could do what game wardens call 'harvesting'. They harvest to reduce the size of a herd of animals when there are too many of a species in one area to be supported by the amount of food available. In this case, reduce the size of your collection by half or two thirds. Afterwards tell everyone that you wanted to share their beauty with others who would enjoy them. And also don't forget to tell them that you are no longer 'collecting' frogs!

If You Love Your Collection

Naturally, the above strategy doesn't apply if your collection is your pride and joy. It may still be clutter in the eyes of others, but as long as you enjoy it, don't worry what others may think. You can make it easier to maintain your collection (and to keep it contained) by putting it in a display case so it doesn't get dusty and dirty.

CUPBOARDS AND DRAWERS
How to organize cupboards and drawers

Organized vs Neat

Being neat is entirely different from being organized. An alphabetized kitchen with everything in order is neat as a pin but totally disorganized. It's how you use something and not its relative position in the alphabet that matters when organizing. There are few absolutes. We're going to offer you some conventional wisdom and guidelines on the subject of organizing cupboards and drawers. You may decide to ignore our advice. That's fine. Follow your instincts and use a unique system of your own. If your system works correctly, you'll be getting the most storage possible from your available space. In addition, you'll be able to locate things easily and can tell at a glance what you're about to run out of. However, no system will work if no one else knows about it or if you can't find things when you need them.

Cupboards

We're going to talk about cupboards first, then drawers. Much of what applies to cupboards also applies to drawers, so read both sections even if you're only interested in organizing the latter. Also, since there are more cupboards and drawers in the kitchen than in any other room, we'll use the kitchen for most of our examples. But use these ideas for organizing cupboards and drawers no matter where they're located in your home.

Like Items Together?

In general, most organizers advise you to organize within drawers and cupboards by like item. That's not entirely helpful. I mean, how many like items do you have? Take a bag of sugar, for example. Nothing else in your kitchen is exactly 'like' a bag of sugar. So the first step in organizing is to strrrrrrretch the normally accepted definition of 'like items'. You may decide that a bag of flour is like a bag of sugar because they are both a basic foodstuff. It would be just as correct if I decide to store the sugar with the coffee. They seem more alike to me because I think of them together. Some people might store the cornflakes next to the sugar. After all, they're both dry and can be packaged in a similarly shaped box. You get the idea. *Make associations that make sense to you.*

Here are some conventional ideas for grouping similar items. Store basics such as flour and sugar together, tinned goods together, then soups and other sub-divisions together within that group. Rice, dried beans, macaroni, and spaghetti may belong together. Put packaged preparations such as salad-dressing and tomato ketchup together. In cupboards full of dishes, it's usually easy to store like items together. Even then, don't forget to stretch the meaning of like items if it suits you. For example, you don't have to store the water glasses in the same cupboard with the coffee mugs if the coffee maker is on the other side of the room. Locate the coffee mugs in a cupboard close to the coffee maker instead.

You may decide to store items together that aren't alike but are used together. If you've taken up Chinese cooking, store all that gear together. If you have several favourite meals, you can store the items used to make each meal together. Or group together all the tools and supplies you use when you barbecue. Or put all the polishes, cleaners, cloths, and sponges for the car together in the bucket you use.

Once you've decided on the like items that go together, then what? Do you leave the rest of the cupboard empty once you run out of like items? Obviously not, but you need to stretch the definition of like items even further to decide which items go next to a completed group of similar items (e.g. what goes next to the flour and the sugar). Here's another place where your first impulse can guide you. Pick things to go together within a cupboard or drawer that seem logical to you. And consider frequency of use and size of the items as you make your decisions. Let's talk about frequency first.

Prime Storage
There is a pecking order among the shelves in a cupboard. As we said in discussing Rule 3, 'hot' items go in 'hot' spots. Prime storage space is the most visible and easiest place to store or retrieve something. It is most definitely not a prime storage spot if getting a certain item in or out of it can throw your back out for a week. For example, my mother stores her Hoover in a spot that's so inaccessible that she practically has to move the television to get it out. The shelves at eye level are prime storage space, and the ones progressively higher or lower are less and less desirable. The same goes for drawers. Top drawers are prime, and the lowest drawer is the least appealing as a storage place. In the kitchen and bathroom, you can even use the worktop itself as prime storage space.

Your job is to match the things you use most often with prime storage areas. For example, ready-to-use foods such as cereals should have a prime location. So should the things you use every day, such as plates, glasses, pots, and pans. The dedicated soufflé casserole or the special pot you use once a year for your not-yet-world-famous chilli should not. But also take a hard look at some of the appliances you leave out. When was the last time you used the fourteen-speed turboblender? If it was months ago, put it and any other similarly neglected appliances away in 'cooler' storage.

Organize only by function, and try not to consider form. Don't leave on the worktop a set of canisters full of things you seldom use, even if they look nice there. They just add to the clutter. If you don't use the things in them very often, put them in a lower or a higher cupboard. But if you really love your canister set and don't want to store it out of sight, use the canisters to store biscuits, nuts and other family favourites – and ignore the labels 'flour', 'sugar', 'coffee', and 'tea' printed on their sides. (Or turn the labels to the wall.)

Size Counts, Too

The height or bulk of an item is the final factor to consider. You do so for the same reason you position shorter people in the front row of a group photo – so you can see all the people in the picture. The payoff is that you don't have to move half the items stored on a particular shelf in an attempt to find what you're looking for. If you store tall and bulky items in the back and progressively shorter things toward the front, you can see at a glance what you're looking for. This is more difficult than it sounds, because the items you're organizing may not differ enough in height. There are also some ideas for solving this problem under 'Anticlutter Equipment'.

You can vary this directive if you own many tall items and just a few short ones. Store tall things in the back and on one or both sides of the cupboard, and reserve only the middle area for short things.

Spices

Ever notice how easy it is to find a particular spice at the supermarket? They are arranged alphabetically on a shelf that allows you to see each spice container easily. Arrange yours in a similar way or on a lazy Susan. For more help on this subject, see the section 'Anticlutter Equipment'.

Drawers

Drawers tend to disintegrate into chaos quickly. One reason for this unhappy event is that drawers have a kind of automatic self-packing design. Every time someone slams a drawer shut, everything in that drawer goes flying to the back of the drawer. Unless that stuff is rearranged to the front regularly, after a while it becomes unused and forgotten. In effect, what's in the back is really only useful for keeping the things in the front from sliding farther back. In addition, you can pack more things into drawers than is wise because what's in it won't fall out when you open it (assuming you *can* still open it), as it would if you loaded a cupboard the same way. All the more reason to try to get the drawers organized.

Follow the same strategies we discussed for cupboards. Start by trying to organize like items together. Put the most frequently used items in the prime top drawers. Many of the things you store in drawers are utensils with handles, and it's hard to recognize each utensil by the handle alone. You can make it easier to spot what you're looking for by storing the handles toward the back of the drawer. Now it's easy to see the difference between a spatula or a serving spoon that have a similar handle.

Drawers – and not just the silverware drawer – need dividers. This applies to drawers full of cooking utensils, linen, and even junk. Dividers keep things organized, save you time locating items, and keep things from compressing to the back of the drawer.

DUPLICATES

Some things you actually need more of!

It's hard to admit, in a book about controlling clutter, that we want you to haul more things into the house.

Duplicates of certain things, however, can save you time and make your life less cluttered and more in control.

Humorist, raconteur, and wit Art Buchwald is quoted as saying, 'The one item you need to complete a chore is downstairs when you are upstairs, and upstairs when you are downstairs.' Whether you have stairs or not, if this type of problem arises regularly, you should consider duplicating certain items to solve it and to make your life a bit simpler.

Vacuuming is usually not that difficult a job. Getting the vacuum cleaner itself out of storage or hauling it up and down stairs can be the annoying and tiring part of the job. We have already recommended that you store the vacuum in a convenient place. But if you have an upstairs and a downstairs to vacuum, consider acquiring an upstairs and a downstairs vacuum. If other areas pose a problem – such as near the door from the garden – a hand-held portable vacuum may be just the thing. (Keep it near the problem area, not away in a cupboard.)

If you're like many people, when you're in the bathroom and getting ready to go somewhere, you're quite interested in what time it is so you won't be late. And it's one of the least likely rooms to have a clock! So add one. A travel clock that you'll use occasionally on trips only costs about £5. It reduces stress, and it saves you from having to leave the room to go somewhere else to check the time.

Several small items are easily and inexpensively duplicated. Put scissors in the kitchen, in your desk, and in your bathroom. Put fingernail clippers in your handbag and a bathroom cupboard or drawer. Put a folding umbrella under the driver's seat in the car. It will avoid all those infuriating times when it starts raining and you don't have an umbrella with you – despite the fact that you own half a dozen of them.

A loose (unmarked) house key in your pocket guarantees that you won't have a real emergency on your hands if you lose your entire ring of keys. At least you can get into the house again.

This is far from a comprehensive list. You'll think of other things that always seem to be in the wrong place. That's the acid test. If you need something that always seems to be in the wrong place, consider duplicating it – especially if it's inexpensive.

FILING CABINETS

How to set up a household filing cabinet

Many desks have one or more drawers designed to accept suspension files. If you're considering purchasing both a desk *and* a filing cabinet, select the desk first: You may find one that has a built-in filing cabinet.

If you have a desk, position your new filing cabinet next to it. The cabinet should be sited so you can open and close the drawers without moving your desk chair.

An indispensable component of a filing system is a set of hanging folders. Hanging folders ride on two metal lugs – one on either side of the folder. Each lug hooks over a thin metal side rail, which enables the hanging folder to slide easily. Most filing cabinets have these rails built in.

Setting up a Filing System

In general, file according to use, not strictly in alphabetical order. For example, put the files you use most often in the front of the top drawer. Examples are files that you work with on an on-going basis – the 'Bills' file you use regularly to pay, and the Building Society/Bank file you remove when you balance your cheque-book against your statement. Continue towards the back of the drawer with files you use less and less often – such as old tax returns or insurance polices you seldom review. Put bulky, seldom-used files in the very back of the drawer where they are harder to get to or remove – especially if you have a filing cabinet whose drawers don't fully extend. For example, I put all the photos that haven't made it into an album yet in this back file. I can open the drawer far enough to stuff more photos into it, and that big, bulky file helps keep the other files in front, where they belong.

Once you have a number of files, it can become difficult to continue filing according to use. In this case, a combination of both usage and the alphabet can be helpful – that is, alphabetize when you get to the seldom-used files, and keep the 'hot' files near the front in order of usefulness.

Now it's time to start deciding how to divide up all the items you have into separate files. We've listed some ideas below, but you don't have to make any final decisions yet. First gather all the things you want in the cabinet. Put that stuff into separate stacks you plan on storing as separate files. Suspension files come in two thicknesses: standard (which holds up to ¾ inch or so of papers) or wide-bottom (which holds up to 2 inches or so of papers). If you try to overstuff the standard files, the contents will start to stick out of the top and get frayed when the drawer opens and closes. Overstuffed files also make it difficult to see the identifying tags for the other files.

As you sort, if one stack gets bigger than 2 inches, find a way to divide it again, and turn it into two or more smaller stacks. For example, if all your bills thrown into a single file will be too jammed, establish a separate file, 'Credit Card Bills', and put the rest of the bills in a second file, 'Bills'. Print a very short description on the paper label and insert it into the plastic tab that comes with the suspension files. The plastic tab has two wings that attach to the suspension file by inserting them one wing at a time into a slot at the top of the suspension file. Stagger these labels by inserting the tabs into different

slots so you can see them all when you open the drawer.
Keep a few extra files, with blank tabs already inserted,
at the back of the filing cabinet. That will make it much
more likely you'll actually start a new file, when needed,
rather than add to a pile of clutter elsewhere.

Some Ideas for File Names

- Archives: Wills, insurance polices, other important
  papers (many of which will be duplicates of the orig-
  inals in a safe-deposit box, if you have one)
- Articles: These are articles you haven't read yet. For
  articles you want to keep after reading, file them in
  their own file by subject (e.g., 'Garden')
- Bank statements
- Bills
- Car
- Catalogues
- Correspondence
- Coupons
- Diskettes
- Humour: This is one you'll enjoy revisiting
- Individuals (by name): One file for each household
  member
- Instruction Manuals
- Personal
- Photographs: Photos before they get installed in an
  album

- Product Information
- Reminders: Paperwork for items listed on the calendar or in your diary (e.g. paperwork for the renewal of the car's tax) invitations for the month so you'll have the address and time handy, and appointments for the month
- Savings Account(s)
- School Papers
- Stamps
- Stationery
- Tax
- Things to Do
- Things to File: If you find yourself being indecisive about where to file something, pop it in here; just don't let it get out of hand – review its contents regularly

If you have room, unorthodox things such as spare batteries, rolls of tape, and pens and pencils all fit nicely into files. It makes it easy to remember where such items are because you can file them by name. You can even file books such as a dictionary or photograph albums that you want to keep close at hand. Be imaginative and you'll get the most out of this file. Notice, however, that there is no 'Miscellaneous' file. That can work too much like a junk drawer. If you decide to have one, keep it small and weed it regularly.

As with organizing cupboards, drawers, wardrobes, etc., we encourage you to follow your first impulses for creating files: they are apt to serve you better than our ideas if ours don't seem to 'fit'. The test of the system is to be able to retrieve something again – not where or under what name you have it filed. So give files names that have an immediate association for you.

Most office workers put the papers for each file into one or more manila folders and then put the manila folders into the suspension file. There are several good reasons for doing this. It's easier to take just one manila folder in and out of your file than the suspension file itself. In addition, you'll always know where to replace the manila folder because the suspension file with its identifying tag is still in place. Moreover, the manila folders enable you to split a suspension file into convenient sub-categories. For example, in the 'car' file you might have separate manila folders for 'Receipts', 'Estimates', 'Instructions', and 'Documents'. Or you can separate the 'Bills' file into its individual components ('Telephone', 'Gas', 'Electricity', 'Water', etc.). You'll know when the suspension file gets too complex to handle without manila folders: you'll be rummaging too much.

If You Have No Desk

If you're using the dining room table as your desk and the filing cabinet isn't close to that table, put an expandable file folder in the front of your cabinet. In it put all the files you use regularly: 'Bills', 'Appointments', 'Current

Account', etc. When it's time to pay bills or balance your current account, remove the entire expandable folder and take it to the dining room table. You now have all the necessary files with you to complete the task at hand without making exasperating trips back to the filing cabinet.

A Calculator

As long as you've gone this far, get a calculator – a real one that disgorges a paper output. It saves time and aggravation and is indispensable when you're balancing your bank account. If you're like most of us, you don't much care for that chore – especially since it never seems to balance on the first or second try. It's amazing how much faster you'll be able to find *your* error (sorry) when you can see the calculations on paper. It's very difficult to find mistakes in, or even trust, totals you can't double-check visually.

GARAGE SHELVES

Assuming garage shelves will not prevent easy access to your car, there is immense scope for useful storage space in a garage. Ready-made shelves with the necessary fittings and instructions are available from DIY stores and the erection of them should cause little difficulty. DIY manuals also deal with the construction of shelves so details are not given here. However, here are a few tips:

1   Shelves should not be less than 18 mm thick for heavy items.

2   Use shelves approximately 12–15 inches wide. Deeper shelves make for inefficient storage as frequently you can neither see nor reach what is at the back.

3   If you want to accommodate larger items such as a dustbin on the floor leave a larger space below the first shelf. Otherwise a first shelf located some 20 inches from the ground is recommended.

4   Measure some of the things to be stored: this will help you decide how far apart to put the shelves. We suggest that, in general, the lower two shelves should be about 15 inches apart and the higher ones 12 inches apart.

5   For ease of working erect the top shelf first.

Storage for Garden Tools Etc

Unless you can store all your garden tools elsewhere a wall of your garage can be most useful. Fix a batten on to the wall and then screw on hooks to fit each article such as hoe, rake, fork, spade, brush etc. You will need about one foot between the hooks for each tool but if you have insufficient space stagger the height of the tools and you can probably manage with about six inches per tool.

For very long items such as pieces of wood or pipe fit

three large shelf brackets above all your other shelves and store the items on the brackets.

HOUSEHOLD CLEANING SUPPLIES
What do you really need?

If you've got household cleaners stuck under sinks, in the garage, and maybe in a storage cupboard or two, most of those cleaners are nothing but clutter – especially if you have cleaners you've never even tried or that haven't seen the light of day in years. We have some very definite ideas about cleaners as items of clutter. We ought to: we use them all day long to clean about fifteen thousand homes a year.

First of all, it makes much more sense to have one cleaner that does ten different jobs than to have ten different cleaners to do ten different jobs. Besides cluttering up the house with all those specialized cleaners, it takes more time and more money to purchase them originally, it's more complicated to replace them as you use them up, and the cleaning job itself takes longer when you're using different kinds of cleaners. How much better, simpler, and more efficient to carry just a few very good ones. We carry just one heavy-duty cleaner and one light-duty cleaner with us as we clean. For example, our heavy-duty liquid cleaner (we call it 'Red Juice') is the best cleaner we've ever come across. It's non-toxic, odourless, and biodegradable. The most important thing, though, is that it works miracles on dirt, grease, and grime in every imaginable combination.

We believe that cleaning supplies should be stored in their own eye-level storage space whenever possible. It's so much simpler to retrieve cleaners and replace them after use from such a cabinet than from the dark and crowded dungeon under the kitchen sink. That's one reason some of us never get around to cleaning: it's too much trouble to get the cleaners out of their hiding places. Many of us don't even know what's under there. Move the cleaners to 'hotter' storage space and use the area under the sink for items you don't often use, or dedicate it to a rubbish bin only. As we're cleaning, we carry our cleaners around the house in a special cleaning apron so we don't make numerous trips back and forth to this storage area.

KEYS

How to avoid searching for the keys every time you want to leave the house

This plan solves the problem of an absolutely needless and particularly exasperating waste of time. And it solves it so effortlessly that it may give you a bit of encouragement to tackle some of the more difficult clutter or organizational problems you're faced with.

All you have to do is mount a screw-in hook (or hooks, if others in the family need help also) close to where you normally end up when you're coming into the house. For many people, that's the kitchen. Or just inside the garage door into the house, or next to the burglar alarm. Usually the second choice of where to mount it is near where you exit – that is, just inside the door rather than where you usually head to in the house after entering. The drawback to leaving the key here is that often you have your arms full of groceries or something else as you enter the house so you can't put your key on its hook until after you set down your load. Now you have to walk back to your entrance point to deposit the key. Ultimately, where you install it is secondary. That it's convenient and actually used is what's important.

If the hook is going to withstand daily assaults, it's got to be mounted into something solid. Were it to come loose in a few days, with the track record some of us have, it might be a year before it's reinstalled. Try putting it directly into the moulding around the door to the kitchen, for example. To avoid splitting the wood and to make it easier to install, pre-drill a hole slightly smaller than the hook. Don't put the hook directly into a door, even if the door is solid wood, because the keys will go flying when the door is opened or closed.

Some gift shops carry a wooden plaque with hooks for hanging keys. It may not be something that your decorator would choose, but that's an even easier option for key management if you do find one you like.

If you have problems finding your keys even after you've put up a key hook, you've probably installed the hook in the wrong place. Move it to a place you can't avoid when entering the house with the keys still in your hand. Consciously develop the habit of using the hook and it will become second nature.

LETTERS

Catching up on correspondence

Household correspondence is best kept in its own file, of course, in chronological order or whatever other order makes sense for your needs (see 'Filing Cabinets', page 90). But are you postponing writing letters to track down that magazine subscription that never came in the mail, or to complain about a defective product, or to commend that bus driver who was especially nice the other day? If so, and if you feel you don't have the time to deal with your correspondence adequately, then you might consider 'standard' letters.

By 'standard' we mean letters that are already substantially pre-written so that sentences or paragraphs can be incorporated in chunks from one letter to another. For example, if you often find yourself writing to order an item by mail, you can set up a standardized letter and use it over and over again for different correspondents. Just change the date, salutation, address, etc. They're especially useful for writing to your local councillor and MP. You don't have to scrounge around for their address every time you write, so you can pop off a letter of furious indignation with an ease that will startle your representatives. If you have a personal computer you can conveniently keep this information in the memory or on a disk.

If you don't want to take the time, or if you want help composing your correspondence, consider investing in one of the books containing standardized letters on all subjects. Use the letters as is, or modify them for your own application. We won't tell a soul where you acquired your newfound literary skills.

MAILING LISTS
Dealing with unwanted mail

Mention unsolicited (mistargeted or 'junk') mail and you'll almost invariably hear a chorus of complaints. I maintain that it's not all that much of a bother. Personally, I enjoy getting all sorts of mail – even mail I didn't request or expect. And the number of direct-mail pieces we receive each day is far outweighed by the number of TV, radio, magazine, and billboard ads we see and/or hear in the same period. Most of us have ordered something via the mail at least once.

In practice it is impossible to stop all unsolicited mail but you can at least indicate, when you fill up a wide variety of coupons, application forms etc. that you do not wish your name to be included on mailing lists. The important thing is to take an immediate decision every time a piece of junk mail lands on your doormat: discard it or take prompt advantage of the 'free' offer or whatever! You can reduce the amount of unsolicited mail you receive by telephoning or writing to the Mail Preference Service, Freepost 22, London W1E 7EZ (0345 034599). They cannot, however, prevent unaddressed leaflets, or unsolicited mail being sent to you from companies that can classify you as a customer. You must contact the company directly.

MEDICINE CABINETS

What's lurking behind the mirror?

For some reason, medicine cabinets often function as a final resting place for objects. This is perfectly understandable, because all sorts of musty things can be hidden behind the mirror. But when the time comes for organizing it, here are a few ideas.

Medicines

Fearlessly grab hold of every medicine bottle, pillbox, tube, can etc with an expiry date that has passed and throw away everything except prescribed medicines. In the case of these retain them until you have compiled a medical history from the labels. There are valid reasons for keeping a medical history. With it, for example, you can tell a doctor which medicines have and have not worked for you in the past. Or it may be necessary to renew a prescription at some point in the future.

Transfer the pertinent information to a summary file record. Keep this file in your household filing cabinet. And record information in a table that looks something like this:

Patient	Date of Prescription	Name & Dose	For	Doctor	Name & Address of Pharmacist
Dad	12/1/91	Voltaren 75 mg. 2x/day	Muscle pain	H. Friedman	J. Smith Swansea

If appropriate, write a note next to the medicines indicating such things as effectiveness, side effects, or cost.

Once you've transferred this information to the table, throw the bottles etc away. You're never going to find something to put in them, and if you throw them out you won't be tempted to store aspirin in a bottle labelled 'Decongestant'.

Fragrances

The next most populous items in the medicine cabinet are likely to be all those half-empty bottles and cans of cologne, perfume, and aftershave you cannot bear to part with. The trouble is – in addition to the lack of shelf space – if you keep them longer than their shelf life, you'll be flouncing about in public with rancid odours wafting from your otherwise delightful self. Fragrances have a shelf life of about one year after being opened. After a year, they begin to sour as the formula oxidizes in the bottle. Unopened, they may last two years. Lower temperatures slow down the rate of chemical breakdown of the fragrance, so refrigerated fragrances can last up to three years. It's also best to keep fragrances out of direct or indirect sunlight. So fragrances left out – especially near a window – are prime candidates for early souring.

Throw away bottles of fragrance you know you've had beyond their shelf life. And don't keep any more than you'll be able to use by the time they're due to sour.

Toiletries

The shelf life of toiletries ranges from six months to several years. Eye cosmetics (e.g., mascara) have the shortest life span. Cosmetics with less water (e.g., lipstick) can last much longer. A shelf life of several years can be expected for toiletries such as mouthwash, tooth-paste, Vaseline, shampoo, hair spray, suntan lotion, and surgical spirit. Some newer lines of products indicate the 'use by' date on the product container itself.

No matter what the product, certain precautions will

ensure the maximum storage life for the product. As discussed above for fragrances, store the toiletry item, wherever practical, in a dark and cool place. Wash your hands before dipping into an ointment, for example, that's going to be around awhile. Items mixed with saliva (e.g., mouthwashes drunk from the bottle, or eye cosmetics moistened with saliva) are naturally going to go bad a bit sooner. Items whose containers are left open and exposed to the air are also going to go around the bend that much quicker. Signs of decay include rancid odour, oil separation, flaking, and discoloration – although discoloration by itself doesn't mean the product has expired (especially for sunscreens).

Once you've removed out-of-date items from the medicine cabinet, take aim at the newer but still unused ones, such as the greasy hair treatment that nobody in the household uses any more, or the makeup that turned out to be a macabre colour. Items in the medicine cabinet are probably more expensive per square inch than anywhere else in the house, but apply the same uncluttering rules here so you'll end up with things you actually use and enjoy.

Store related items on the same side of the medicine cabinet – especially if it has more than one door. This means that the hairbrush, hair comb, hair spray, hair cream, mousse, hair colour, and hair restorer all go on the same side. Likewise, keep together the contact-lens cleaner, the saline solution, and the lenses' storage case.

Also arrange the two sides with an eye towards the

sequence in which you use the cabinet – especially if there are two or more doors on the cabinet. For example, if you take care of your hair first, then put on deodorant, and then apply a fragrance, store them in a logical sequence in the cabinet so you don't have to switch between sides. Organize what's left according to the guidelines in the section 'Cupboards and Drawers'.

NATIONAL GEOGRAPHICS
They seem to be everywhere

At any one time there may be over 3 billion copies of *National Geographic* in print, and just about every one of them is still in somebody's garage in one country or another. It is such a splendidly photographed thing of beauty that we feel like criminals when we try to throw one away.

But as beloved as they are, the time comes when *National Geographic*s need another home. Be generous. Be wily. Take the plunge. And be comforted by the fact that every issue you have is likely to be in the local library.

Some disposal tips are:

· Donate the magazines or maps to special education and English-as-a-second-language classes.

- Use the magazines or maps as wallpaper for a den, child's room, etc.
- Donate the magazines and/or maps to charity shops.
- Include the maps in your next car-boot sale.
- Donate the maps to geography and history teachers, who love to get their hands on them for use as visual aids in the classroom.

In general, the most likely outlets are schools, libraries, prisons, hospitals, nursing homes and charities.

PAPER

What to do with all the paper that slithers into the house

You'd think that paper clutter would be easy to deal with. After all, paper comes boldly through the front door in broad daylight. It's not surreptitious, like a mouse. Actually, it's probably easier to get rid of the mouse – at least you can set a trap for it.

There's something about the importance of the printed word on paper that causes even the most conscientious among us to put off making a decision. When the mail arrives, we sort through it and then put it in a growing pile, even though we could have disposed of it just about as quickly by deciding appropriately right then and there. The first step is to make the preliminary sorting of incoming post more useful: as soon as you pick it up, throw away what you don't want or aren't interested in into the recycling or rubbish bin – not into a separate stack on the worktop 'for now'. You're not going to experience an unexpected burst of interest in it later.

If you're like the rest of us, there are undoubtedly several bills in your mail most days. Put those in your filing cabinet in the 'Bills' file as you come to them. If a piece of mail was an invitation addressed to you alone, decide then and there if you are going to attend, note it in your diary or mark it on your calendar, and file the invitation in your monthly Reminder, follow-up or tickler file. If the invitation is for you and your spouse, or if it includes the children, put it on the kitchen/dining-room table and get an answer that night at dinner. Then file it appropriately.

If you're lucky enough to get a real letter from a real person, read that correspondence and file it in your correspondence file. Put the interesting ads or magazines next to your chair in the living room and sit down to read them when you can.

If you don't even glance at some of the magazines you subscribe to, save yourself the guilt and the expense and cancel those subscriptions. The magazines coming into the house are chock full of articles that either look interesting to you or that you know you 'should' read. They may make you feel like a failure because you almost never get around to them. Why put yourself through all that? If you cancel them, you'll shed the guilt and save a few pounds a year.

For the magazines you do look at, at least cursorily, tear or cut out interesting articles and recycle the rest of the magazine so you don't have growing piles of them all over the house. Put these saved but unread articles in your filing cabinet in their own file and read them at your leisure – without the clutter of the rest of the magazine. The article file is fun to look through when you have time and are in the mood. You'll find some wonderful articles. But you'll also discover that many of them have since lost their appeal, and those you can discard more easily. Once you've read an article, throw it away, give it to a friend, or file it in one of the permanent files you allow yourself for articles (e.g., 'Cats', 'Diets', 'Garden', etc.).

You will never discard all your correspondence, but when you've answered a card or a letter, generally throw it away. The same goes for Christmas cards. Update your address book as necessary, and recycle the cards. Save those special letters from special people at special times in your life in a separate 'Correspondence' file.

PHOTOGRAPHS
Organizing memories

Here's an effective guide to reducing drawers full of photos. It will reduce those volumes of photos to a number and format that people may actually look at and enjoy. That was the whole idea in the first place, right? You'll not only be able to enjoy the photos again, you'll also be reclaiming all the drawer space they were taking up.

Supplies

1 A table-top or other large working surface.
2 A photo storage unit, or several photo albums of your choice.
3 A video transfer system or service (optional).

The first step is to round up all your photos. As one storage place fills up, people start storing them in a new place, so investigate the house thoroughly. You'll need every last picture at hand to do this properly.

The idea is to edit your photo collection. Think of your photos as raw footage of a film. If all the footage shot to make *Cleopatra* were shown, the audience would expire from boredom. Likewise, your home photo album collection is unedited, and the show is far too long and boring. People just won't look at them if there are too many photos per event. In the first packet of pictures, you may notice that of the thirty-four prints, twenty-seven of them are of your grandchild's second birthday party. Like most people, you have occasional gems interspersed in a much larger collection of more ordinary photos, plus repeats. Let's fix that. While we're fixing it, don't cause any damage to your photos unnecessarily. Keep your hands clean, don't handle the photos more than necessary, and there's no reason even to touch the negatives during this process.

If your collection consists of slides, use a light box that will allow you to view a number of slides at once. You don't need a fancy one: a cheap plastic fold-up model will do. Or you may be able to rent one. Except for how you view them, you'll edit them exactly the same as prints. With slides and home movies, pay particular attention to the video transfer option at the end of this section.

Organize

Once you've gathered together all the packets of photos, start by sorting them into chronological order. If you're lucky, the processing date is on the packets or on the back of the prints. The packets themselves may already be somewhat sorted chronologically by the way they were put in the drawers (i.e. the oldest ones are at the bottom). If this is true in your case, keep them in that same order. If you have absolutely no idea about the year of certain groups of photos, set them aside for now. Start a new pile whenever the one you've been working on gets too tall and unwieldy. Each pile should be arranged so the oldest photos are on top.

Once you've gone through them all, you'll have the photos, some still in their packets, arranged roughly by year. Now it's time to decide where to insert the photos you set aside earlier. After you've seen all the photos, sometimes your memory will be jogged and you'll now know where a stray group belongs. If you still don't know where some photos belong, consult other family members or friends. As a last resort, guess.

Edit

Start with the oldest photos. Go through this first pile, one photo at a time. As you look at each photo, you're going to make an increasingly rapid editorial decision. Do you want to see this again? Do others? If yes, put it in the 'keep' pile. If no, put it on the floor or in a wastepaper basket but not back in the packet. You might as well place an empty wastepaper basket right next to you, because you're going to need it. Save the packets, with negatives enclosed, in chronological order for the time being.

When you come to several photos of one event, you not only have to decide which photos are keeps and which are discards, you also have to pick the best of the keeps. For example, you may have an entire packet of photos of Christmas 1986. Spread them all out on the table. Discard the obvious misses. Now pick the very best photo from those not discarded and put it in the keep pile. Then find the second-best picture on that same subject and put it in a separate 'seconds' pile. Pick a third-best photo on the subject and put it in a separate 'thirds' pile. *Throw away* any additional pictures of that same subject.

Share

Ultimately you'll keep the best photos for yourself and give the seconds and thirds photos to other family members or friends. If there are more than two such people living away from home, make a stack for each of them. If your kids are still at home, make collections of the seconds and thirds and save them for when they're older. Just never tell anyone which ones are seconds and thirds, so siblings never have an inkling that someone is getting preferential treatment. Set all the negatives aside for now, leaving them in their original packet and in chronological order.

By giving photos to people who don't live in your home, you will realize one very important benefit: in case of a disaster such as a fire or a flood, these second and third copies of your precious photos will survive because they've been sent elsewhere.

Let's be very clear by what we mean by saving just the *one* best photo of each subject for yourself. Let's say you have over two dozen perfectly good pictures of the afore-mentioned grandchild's birthday party, but you're going to save only the best one. Please don't start making smaller subjects so you can try to get away with saving more photos – pictures with others in them, pictures of the grandchild alone, pictures of eating, pictures of the games played, pictures opening gifts, etc. Just the best *one*. This child has his or her birthday picture taken by you every year, and you take pictures at Christmas, Easter, Summer holidays, parties, etc. If you keep just one from each of these occasions from birth until 15, you'll have 75 pictures of this one child. That would fill an album. You'll be satisfied.

If you have just one photo of a particular subject, it doesn't mean you can't get rid of it. For photos that are not repeats, ask yourself these questions: Do I know why the picture was taken? (A magnificent sunset, perhaps, but now that you've captured it on film, you realize you had to be there to enjoy it properly.) Do I even know what it is? (It's surprising how many photos are so obscure they're unidentifiable. Perhaps you were going through an arty period with your camera.) Do I know who is in it? (If neither you nor anyone else in the household does, why memorialize them forever by including their photo in your collection?) As you've probably already guessed, throw away these photos.

Similarly, if you took twenty-five photos of the aforementioned sunset and not one of them was any good, don't automatically save a first, second, and third and add them to their respective piles. Instead, throw the whole batch away.

Ultimately you'll have three or so piles left (depending on how many piles you've been making to give away). By far the largest pile should be the one in the wastepaper-basket. Remember *Cleopatra*. Editing reduced the *Cleopatra* footage from hundreds of hours down to two hundred and forty-three minutes. Something similar should happen when you edit your home photos.

Now send the copies to whomever you decided on. The photos you have left are in chronological order, changing subjects as they occurred, and you're all set to put them in the albums. Do it quickly before someone knocks over the piles!

Identify and Display

As long as you've gone to all this trouble to get the photos edited and filed, take one more important step: write the names of the subjects, the location, and the approximate date on the back of each photo you've kept. Most of us have old family photos that no one in the family can identify with certainty. The next generation to enjoy this wonderful album you are making will bless you for taking the time now to add archival information to the back of the photos. If you have slides, movies, or videotapes, make these same annotations.

Another method of displaying your photos is to transfer them to a video format. If you already have the video camera, you can purchase a video transfer system for about £50. This method is especially efficient if your collection is in slide form. It's so much simpler to view them via the VCR than with the slide projector and screen buried in the back of a cupboard somewhere. The same consideration should be given to home movies.

However, there are two disadvantages to transferring to videotape. The first is that you get a somewhat fuzzier image of your slides – not the crisp, sharp image you get from the slide itself. The second disadvantage is that the videotape can be damaged or broken more easily than the slides themselves. Videotape, even unbroken, doesn't last forever and may start to decay after a number of years.

The Negatives

Don't even try to edit the negatives. Just save them all as is. The simplest option is to leave them in their original packets, but number the packets sequentially (starting with 1 for the oldest) while you still have them in order. In the event you ever do duplicate them, you won't have to go through the chronological sorting again. Now put them all in a small box, mark the outside of the box, and put it away in the back of a drawer or cupboard. Better yet, put them in a home safe or a bank safe-deposit box. Alternatively, photographic equipment shops sell translucent storage envelopes for negatives. They allow you to store them in a three-ring binder album or in your filing cabinet. You can identify negatives quickly, without handling them, by holding them up to the light. Remember to transfer any notes or identifying information from the packet to the sheet.

RECIPES

There's an easy way to manage them

What about that mass of random clippings and notes that constitutes your collection of recipes (exclusive of cookery-books)? Driving you batty, eh? You're not alone. A friend of mine has recipes stuffed in cookbooks, half-sorted in envelopes, transferred onto 3- by 4-inch *and* 4- by 6-inch index cards (two different half-finished projects), and floating around on his bookshelves in a permanent holding pattern. (He rarely cooks, by the way.)

The alternative is refreshingly simple and can be used fast enough to lure even the most inveterate of clutterers into becoming more organized with their recipes. Set up fat three-ring binders loaded with plastic sheet protectors. A blank sheet of paper in each protector is a helpful background for the clippings you're about to add. Install divider sheets with tabs on which you have written sage words such as 'Soups', 'Chicken', 'Desserts', and the like.

When a new recipe leaps out at you from Wednesday's newspaper, just pop it into one of the sheet protectors. No tape, no staples, no retyping.

One of the side benefits to this system is that when you turn to the appropriate section, you will probably discover you already had a recipe for Chicken Cacciatore. If the new recipe has an interesting twist, just annotate the existing recipe and throw away the usurper. Or if the newer recipe is a low-fat variation, pop it in the sheet next to the traditional variation.

Another benefit of this system is that you can create some inventive categories for recipes, so you'll end up with your own customized cookbook. For example, you might have a category called 'Romantic', or 'Cheap', or 'Dinner for Two', or 'Fast', or even 'Tofu'.

Yet another benefit is that you can have a section called 'Restaurants'. At last! A place to keep all those stray restaurant reviews. (The alternative is to create a separate file for them in your filing cabinet.)

Provided you don't get carried away, these binders can become Recipe Central for the kitchen – that is, you can refer yourself to cookery-books without rewriting the recipes for the binder. Just keep a handwritten list, in the front of each section, of favourite recipes in various cookery-books. For example, in the front of the 'Desserts' section you might list 'Meyer Lemon Mousse – *Greens Cookery-book*, page 354' without copying out the recipe at all.

If the number of three-ring binders expands beyond

one, make sure you label the spine so you can grab the right binder without the slightest hesitation. Anything that gets in your way might tip the balance in favour of stuffing the recipe in a more slothful place, so be alert.

RECORDKEEPING

Which records to save and how long to save them

You may be storing decades of cheque-book stubs, bank statements, receipts, and assorted slips of paper only because of a morbid fear of the Inland Revenue. Like many of us, you're convinced you'll need all of those records in perpetuity to avoid problems in a tax audit or investigation.

Tax-Related Records You Should Keep

No matter where you derive your income, keep the proofs of its sources. For most employees, it's a P60 form. If your income is from a pension, investments, or other sources, the same holds true: save the tax vouchers and other appropriate pieces of paper.

Then there are the expenses and deductions. We aren't going to delve too deeply into that subject. That's between you, the Inland Revenue, your accountant, and the Supreme Being of your choice. Whatever you claim, however, keep a record of its origins. Keep the receipt, sales slip, or other documents. And get a signed and dated receipt for any cash payments claimed.

How to Organize the Records

Establish a file for the current year. A suitable name for the tax file would be 'Taxation 19–/20–'. In this file put all papers related to income and deductible expenses for this year only. For example, this is the place to put your most recent pay slip or dividend vouchers, as well as any receipts or paid bills that may be deductible. Within this file, put a labelled manila folder or envelope for each type of income and expense.

Keep a separate file ('Property') for documents pertaining to your home or other property. But use the 'Taxation 19–/20–' file for documentation on mortgage interest. File papers in the 'Property' file that contain basic information about your property or that will impact on taxes for more than one year. Use the 'Taxation 19–/20–' file for papers concerned with the current year only.

Besides the Inland Revenue, there's another good reason to organize these records into files. When you die someone else must take care of your estate and you'll save yourself from being cursed in your grave by your survivor, executor, or the administrator of your estate.

Bills, Receipts Etc.

As virtually no UK bank returns cancelled cheques it is important that you retain cheque-book stubs. Also keep paying-in slips, credit-card slips, bank and credit-card statements, bills and receipts particularly insofar as they relate to transactions which have tax implications or to your property or car repairs. Get into the habit of writing the cheque number on all receipts you put in the tax file.

Stationers have inexpensive cardboard boxes that hold hanging files upright, like your filing cabinet does. You could use one of those boxes for all previous years' tax files if your filing cabinet is full. While you're about it, look for other boxes that can be helpful for your particular storage needs. There are specialized cardboard boxes for blankets, dishes, paper records of differing sizes, and many others. It takes up much less storage space when the box you're using is just the right size.

Summarizing Your Tax Receipts

Since clutterers have an innate horror of keeping track of receipts, go easy on yourself. Just pop them into the front of the 'Taxation 19–/20–' file or into a manila folder kept there marked 'Receipts'. Make sure this file is easy to reach: if you have to search for it, your resolve may fail and the receipt will end up in your cheque book, as a bookmark, or in little piles everywhere.

Every so often, sift through these loose receipts in the 'Taxation 19–/20–' file (preferably annotated with the cheque number) and sort them into their respective manila folders or envelopes. How often you do so depends in part on the amount of paperwork your financial affairs generate. Try to sort them monthly (when you pay your bills, perhaps) or at least several times a year.

As long as you're sifting through this fine collection of receipts, it will greatly simplify your life at tax time if you summarize them from time to time.

For those with unusual returns, scrutinize your return from last year to determine what categories to use for your own unique summary. When tax time comes, you'll be able to tally up each column in a flash, making the task of calculating your taxes incomparably more pleasant. If you hire an accountant to prepare your return, you can present these summaries with a flourish and watch him or her burst into tears. One reason for the tears is gratitude; the other is that he or she won't be able to bill as many hours for the preparation of your return.

How Long Should You Keep Your Records

Professionals know reasons for storing documents that mere mortals can barely imagine. They've experienced firsthand the trench warfare of investigations and audits, and they've held the hands of those who've lost money because they were unable to document certain expenses. So we've prepared the following cheery little summary based on the recommendations of accountants and auditors.

Document	Keep
Adoption papers	Forever
Bank records	Six years
Birth certificates	Forever
Contracts	Seven years past expiration
Credit-card records	Six years
Custody agreements	Forever
Death certificates	Forever
Deeds of covenant	Four years past expiration
Divorce decrees	Forever
Health records	Forever
Home-improvement records and bills for major repairs	Until you sell the house
Income tax returns	Forever
Insurance policies	Four years past expiration
Inventory of major personal property	Forever
Investment records	Four years after disposal
Loan papers	Three years after final payment
Marriage certificates	Forever
Medical and National	

Insurance cards	Forever
Mortgage papers	Three years after final payment
Owner's manuals	As long as you own the device or appliance
Passports	Forever (as a record of travel)
Pension documentation, including BR464	Forever
Rent receipts	Treat as tax records if making office-at-home claims
Tax records	Six years after due date
Tax records, if fraudulent or false returns were filed, or if no return was filed (shudder) even though one was due	Eternity
Title deeds	Forever
Utility bills (heating, lighting, telephone, general and water rates)	Treat as tax records if making office-at-home claims
Warranties and guarantees	As long as you own the device or appliance
Wills and codicils	Forever or until superseded by a new will

SHOPPING

Shopping made easy – well, easier

The more efficiently you shop, the fewer trips you'll make to the supermarket and shop. Making unnecessary trips to the shop is a form of disorganization in your life.

Off-Hours

Shop outside normal working hours and early in the week if possible. If you must shop at the weekend, be there when the store opens as it should be easier for service and parking.

It's inconvenient to buy groceries when you have to go to the supermarket after work to buy food for dinner that night – the same predicament many others are in. That's why the store is so busy during those hours, needless to say. Instead, try shopping after dinner the night before. The trip will take you half the time. And you'll buy less food on impulse, shopping on a full stomach!

Work towards a goal of shopping for food only once a week – every other week if you can. The secret is having a complete list when you shop so you don't miss an essential item or purchase unnecessary ones. Also buy in sufficient quantity. Let's talk about the list first.

Lists

Before you go to the supermarket, complete a list. We say 'complete' because you should keep a note pad handy and add items as you become aware of them. Add items you use in quantity to your list when you open the next-to-last one from your supply of that item. Mayonnaise, soap, and paper towels are common examples of what we mean. Don't wait until you open the last one or, needless to say, until you're out. That's the kind of mistake that'll force you to go shopping sooner than you planned.

Pads of paper are cheap. Thoughts are fleeting. So put pads of paper for lists (or ideas about other things you don't want to float away) in several places other than the kitchen. Put one in the bathroom, on the bedside table, in your car, or in your purse. If practical, stop right in the middle of whatever you're doing to add an inspired addition to your list. Otherwise it's too easy to forget. Occasionally round up the lists from the other places and add those items to the master list in the kitchen. It's much easier to complete your list if your cupboards are organized and you can see at a glance what's running low.

Before you go to the supermarket, arrange the list by group – so all the dairy items are together, for example – or by aisle (if you know your supermarket that well). It's too easy to miss items if you rely on the 'cross off each item as you grab it' method.

Whenever you have to go to the shops, be sure you also do anything else that needs attention while you're out and about. That's when those other lists will come in handy: the one in the bathroom about getting another allergy prescription; the one in the bedroom to remind yourself to take the dress to the dry cleaner's for next week's dinner; and the list in the car, where you were when you remembered that the tyres need to be checked. Do all those things on this one trip even though it will take you twice as long. It will take four times as long if you make the trips separately.

Quantity

Buy in quantity. Don't do it to save money, do it so you don't have to run to the shops, fight the traffic and crowds, and miss your favourite TV programme. Don't limit buying in bulk to food items either. You'd be amazed at the number of people in line at the post office who have a stack of envelopes in hand and buy exactly the same number of stamps as envelopes. They post them and leave the post office without a single stamp for a supply at home. I don't understand this behaviour. I *hate* going to the post office. You can never tell when it'll be least crowded. Why would anyone put himself or herself through such time-wasting torture more often than necessary? Any time you find yourself at the front of the line at the post office, buy several months' worth of stamps. Even a year's supply of stamps wouldn't be too much. One hundred stamps cost about the same as a bag of groceries. Stamps never expire, and you can store them safely in your filing cabinet, where you can find them when you need one.

The same goes for greetings cards. Keep an inventory the same way you would keep a supply of stationery for letters. Keep a supply of birthday cards, for example, and resist making innumerable shopping trips for each occasion as it occurs. Don't get carried away: keep only reasonable amounts of extras. Storing three extra deodorants is more akin to the problem than the solution.

Sophisticated Shopping

Sophisticated shoppers start their Christmas shopping in July, August, or any time they come across a bargain or an item that would be just right for someone. The holiday season is entirely too busy a time of year as it is. You'll feel smugly organized if your shopping is at least partially finished by the time it arrives. And rightly so.

When purchasing things for your home, try to imagine how they will look after being pawed by the kids or after sitting out for a few months. For example, consider the following:

· How will it look dusty, dirty, and fingerprinty? Some things look terrible (such as a glass table, or many

small plastic items) unless they are sparkling clean.
· How will you clean it? Some things (baskets are an example) are difficult to dust.

If you ask yourself these questions, you will stop some clutter from ever making it through the front door.

TELEPHONE BOOKS

Be inventive with your telephone directories. Don't just leave them the way they came. Highlight personal and business numbers you use regularly. Annotate wherever you get the impulse (e.g. if the plumber did a great job, scribble a note to yourself so you'll remember the next time).

Install tabs on the edges of important pages. For example, if you find yourself regularly hunting for the page with foreign codes, attach a tab to that page. You don't need fancy ones: You can add a folded-upon-itself piece of transparent tape (a type that will accept ink).

TELEPHONES

How to manage the telephone instead of the other way around

You know how it goes: you think you've finally got a

moment to yourself, and the phone rings. An hour later, when at last you've extricated yourself from the phone, it's too late to finish in the kitchen, start your correspondence, pay bills, or visit the children. So you go to bed, with the unsettling feeling that once again you didn't complete anything close to what you set out to do that day.

If your work requires you to use the phone, you've probably had some training in how to use it. It's only sensible to believe that some things you learned about telephone usage at the office would apply to the home. They do.

Avoiding Interruptions

An answer-phone is essential. Use it even when you're home, at least when you would just as soon not be interrupted or when you want to enjoy some precious peace and quiet. It seems as if the only time a phone isn't answered when people are actually at home is when they're in the middle of something behind closed bedroom doors, and even then they have to stop and think about it for a second. Only in dire emergencies does anyone have the right to demand your attention when you don't want to offer it. You're a busy person, and there is absolutely no need for you to drop everything you're doing every time the phone rings.

Managing your incoming calls doesn't mean you

don't like the person calling, or that you don't think he or she is important. It's just that you have your own agenda, and you'll talk to the person when it's more convenient or when you have the time and enthusiasm to spare.

Some people are reluctant to use an answering machine because they're afraid they might miss an emergency or urgent call. But if you follow that line of reasoning very far, you'll be reluctant to go to the shops or out to dinner for the same reason.

The same goes for important calls. The likelihood of getting such a call is outweighed by the certainty of the aggravation caused by slavishly answering every call. Besides, we're not saying that you won't return such calls promptly. All the messages are right there on your machine, and you can check them at will.

For total privacy, unplug the phone and turn down the volume of the answering machine. You can even put the answering machine on a pillow so you don't hear the 'clunk' when it responds to a call. Obviously, an intermediate level of privacy is made possible by screening incoming calls. If someone calls whom you want to speak to, pick up the call and turn off the machine. Most people seem to be flattered if you do pick up. If you don't, they won't know if you're at home anyway.

If the location of your answering machine is such that you have to go flying across the house to monitor it, consider having other phone points installed so you can move your answering machine to more convenient locations. For example, a point near the door to the back garden can be very handy.

Terminating Calls

When you do answer your calls, it's no crime whatsoever to tell whoever is calling that you're in the middle of something – or that you're just about to leave – and that you'll call him or her back. It's also nice to say when you'll call back. In fact, try to make all your calls at your convenience.

Naturally, you should vary these tactics to end a personal call if the caller keeps on gabbing. Traditionally, whoever calls is supposed to give the conversational signal that the call is coming to an end. But if that doesn't happen, speak your mind without feeling it's a confrontation. Just say the truth: it's time for you to go. Even if a caller is particularly insecure, most can survive a gentle reminder of the realities (and the pressures) of time.

If you don't want to take calls and don't want a message on the answering machine because of other household members, just ask them to take a message for you. There's no need to lie. But tell them exactly what to say: 'Mum can't come to the phone right now. Can I take a message?' Or 'Dad's in the middle of something. Can he call you back?'

If you don't want to listen to a sales call, don't feel bad about ending it. As soon as you know what type of call it is, interrupt, and in a calm voice say, 'I'm sorry, but I'm not interested.' Quietly hang up if the caller persists. Remain cool. But also note that you may have to interrupt the caller to get your message across. Take charge of the situation, end it quickly and with civility, and get back to whatever you were doing – unruffled. Since it seems impossible to stop these unsolicited interruptions, at least you've wasted the least amount of time because you don't have a long cool-down period before you can get back to what you were doing.

If, by chance, it's Mother Teresa herself calling for a contribution, ask her to mail the literature to you, give her your address (if she doesn't already have it), congratulate her on her fine work, then say good-bye and quietly hang up.

Mobility

Get a cordless telephone. It's a magnificent invention. You can stir the pot on the stove, move to a more comfortable spot, let the dog out, answer the front door, and relax on the patio all during the same phone conversation. This is what we all tried to accomplish with long cords, remember? Those were the cords that were so tangled they became functionally shorter than the ordinary ones. When they weren't tangled, they were stretched across the room so people were forever tripping over them and sending the phone flying. The cordless phone overcomes these drawbacks effortlessly.

As long as no one 'improves' this phone by adding a picture so the other person can see what you're really up to, we think it's well worth the investment. And the latest models are substantially improved in performance from the earlier ones.

If your budget won't allow a cordless phone, at least move your phone or add an extension phone so it's conveniently located. If you have a phone at your desk, for example, you can often be doing other things while you're on interminable hold.

VIDEOTAPES

Reel storage solutions

Videotapes can clutter a living room or entertainment area in no time – especially if you get behind in labelling them and if you're taping programmes far beyond a human being's reasonable capacity to watch them. Here are a few steps you can take to straighten out the cassette mess.

This anti-clutter project involves a couple of technical considerations to be observed. First, videotapes (and audiotapes, for that matter) should not be shelved or stored flat for any length of time – the spool of tape should be positioned vertically. After a few days, tape stored flat can settle on the spool unevenly – especially the outer edges – due to gravity.

If the tape is loaded unevenly on the spool, it may be fed across the heads of the VCR unevenly as well. This can cause the playback picture to deteriorate in quality or to disappear altogether.

Luckily, if the tape has become uneven, there's a simple solution: 'repack' the tape by fast-forwarding it and rewinding it back to the beginning. This will re-spool the tape in an even manner. Repacking loads the tape to the exact tension at which your particular machine operates, so the quality of the recording will be at its optimum. Indeed, manufacturers recommend that new tape should always be fast-forwarded and then rewound before the first recording.

The second technical consideration is that tape in storage is vulnerable to all sorts of things: moisture, dust, sunlight, heat, etc. Moisture is especially nasty for tapes. When moist, the tape's surface emulsion softens and can be literally scraped off when the tape passes over the VCR heads. Not only are the heads clogged (they can be easily cleaned) but the tape can be permanently damaged as well.

The solution is to store videotapes, when not in use, in airtight cases. The least expensive option is to be diligent about putting the tape back into the cardboard (or preferably plastic) sleeve that originally came with the tape. Such sleeves leave one side exposed to the elements, but unless you park them next to an open window or shower, you're probably not doing any significant damage to the tape. Video engineers are rather hard to pin down on this subject, however.

The preferred option –and the one selected by just about every video professional – is to store recorded tape in airtight plastic cases. These will protect tapes from deteriorating influences as well as anything short of storing them in a vacuum. In addition, they offer the advantage of making the tapes uniform in appearance on the shelf. Tapes tucked away in a drawer present no aesthetic dilemma, but they can look disorderly on an open exposed shelf unless stored in uniform cases. The one drawback of video storage cases (besides the slight added expense) is that they may be too wide to fit into a storage rack you may already have. But once in cases, tapes stand on their own more easily (like books), so a rack may not be needed.

The speed of deterioration of the tape also depends on the quality of the tape as well as the conditions of storage. Naturally, the cheaper the tape (in general) the faster the deterioration. Again, it's hard to be specific – but if your tape is over seven years or so old, it's in the danger zone. The 'pro' lines of tape will usually last longer, but even they must eventually be transferred to fresh tape after several years. Unfortunately, the way to tell is almost always after the fact. When you play a tape that's too old, you'll behold a virtually immediate, massive, and stomach-wrenching clogging of the heads as the old emulsion is scraped off by the heads.

The next task for decluttering your videotapes, now that you have them repacked and possibly ensconced in cases, is to label them. We all know how easy it is to amass a pile of tapes that have any number of movies or programmes recorded on them, but we somehow didn't stop to label them and now nobody has the foggiest idea what's on them. It's too much of an ordeal to replay the tapes, so we set them aside and start in on new ones. Not only is this an expensive habit but also the shelves are bulging at the seams with unidentified tapes.

There are several steps you can take to make headway here. First, have a stack of Post-Its (or something similar) and a pencil right next to the VCR. When you start the recording, stick the Post-It on the VCR itself or the tape case to remind you of the programme. Then just slap the Post-It on the tape case as you eject the tape from the VCR. If it's a recording you want to keep indefinitely, transfer the information to the tape's own label.

If you record several programmes or films on one tape, be systematic about how you're going to find the beginning of each segment. We all know how annoying it is to scan through the tapes – not to mention the needless wear and tear that's being added to the machine. We suggest you write down, on the label, the start time of each segment (e.g. 20:32) ensuring, of

course, that the time counter is at zero when you begin
the recording.

Appendix: Products List

The past few years have seen a proliferation of devices to help you combat clutter. Your local B & Q, Homebase, etc., have a wide range as do good department stores. We're a bit nervous about listing them as it is important to remember that these gadgets should be used for storing and organizing items that are left over *after* you've uncluttered your home. Don't use them to store stuff you shouldn't keep in the first place! Keep the Uncluttering Rules in mind at all times as you sally forth into this domain.

A few suggestions are:

- Pot-lid racks
- Under-shelf baskets
- Spice racks
- Cork memo strips

- Tie organizers
- Coat/hat hooks
- Under-bed storage chests
- Silver drawer-liners
- Shoe racks
- Jewellery cases
- Shower shelves
- Towel racks
- Laundry bins
- Document storage boxes
- Stackable storage bins
- Videotape racks
- Audio cassette racks
- Photo albums
- Print/negative cases